W9-CON-445

AMERICA'S FAVORITE
FOOD

AMERICA'S FAVORITE
FOOD

Alex Barker

Gramercy Books
New York

This 2003 edition is published by
Gramercy Books, an imprint of
Random House Value Publishing, a
division of Random House, Inc.,
New York.

Gramercy is a registered trademark and
the colophon is a trademark of
Random House, Inc.

Random House
New York•Toronto•London•Sydney•
Auckland
www.randomhouse.com

Printed and bound in Italy

All photography supplied by
Food Features

A catalog record for this title is
available from the Library of Congress.

ISBN 0-517-21845-3

10 9 8 7 6 5 4 3 2 1

CONTENTS

APPETIZERS

SHRIMP COCKTAIL

A shrimp cocktail is one of the most popular ways to start a meal and varies hugely from coast to coast. The sauce can be a spiced and slightly tangy tomato mix like this one or something seriously hot and fiery. Add horseradish for that unmistakeable background kick, mayonnaise for a smooth creamy finish, avocado to cool the whole thing down, or chili to pep it up. It's up to you.

Serves 4

INGREDIENTS:
1/2 cup tomato ketchup
1 tsp Worcestershire sauce
Juice of 1/2 lime
Salt and black pepper
1 clove of garlic, crushed
1/2 iceberg lettuce, shredded
2–3 scallions, washed and chopped
At least 6 large tiger shrimp per person (or about 10 oz smaller ones), cooked
Wedges of lemon to serve

PREPARATION:
1. Mix together the first five ingredients for the sauce and chill until required. If you wish, partly shell the large tiger shrimp, leaving the tails on to make them easier to pick up.

2. Arrange the shredded lettuce and scallions in 4 glass serving dishes or sundae glasses. Top with the shrimp, a little of the sauce, and a wedge of lemon.

3. Place the rest of the sauce in a bowl for passing around.

CREAMY CRAB MOUSSE (right)
This is light and airy and can be made using crab, lobster or large shrimp.

Serves 4

INGREDIENTS:
3/4 cup cooked white crabmeat
2 tbsp light cream
2 tbsp good bought mayonnaise
1/2 tbsp lemon juice

1 tsp chopped fresh dill
Salt and black pepper
1 tsp powdered gelatin dissolved in 2 tsp very hot water
1 large egg white

PREPARATION:
1. In a bowl, mix together the crabmeat, cream, mayonnaise, lemon juice, dill, and seasoning to taste. Cover and chill.

2. Make sure the gelatin is thoroughly dissolved and quite clear either by placing it in a microwave on high for 10-second bursts, or leaving it over a pan of simmering water for a few minutes. Cool slightly, then gently stir the gelatin into the fish mixture.

3. Whisk the egg white until it is stiff and stands in peaks, then carefully fold into the crab-gelatin mixture.

4. Spoon the mixture into a small terrine or individual ramekins and chill for 1–2 hours. Serve with Melba toast or warm fresh bread.

NEW ENGLAND CLAM CHOWDER (overleaf)
There are many arguments as to which is the original and best version of clam chowder: the creamy New England or the tomato-based Manhattan. This is the New England recipe, which was originally a much simpler dish, made from whatever fish was available and thickened with bread or broken crackers. With the addition of milk, cream and potatoes it has evolved into the dish we know today.

Serves 4–5

INGREDIENTS:
48 medium clams in their shells or the equivalent canned
4-oz piece salt pork or thick slice of bacon, finely chopped
1 1/2 tbsp sunflower oil
1 onion, chopped
2 cloves of garlic, crushed
Black pepper
2 tsp fresh thyme leaves
4 medium potatoes, chopped (peel if you wish)
1 1/4 cups milk

1¼ cups light cream
Chopped fresh parsley to serve

PREPARATION:

1. Prepare the clams by scrubbing them thoroughly under fresh running water. Place in a large pan with 1 inch of water. Simmer, covered, for 4–5 minutes or until the shells open up. Discard any shells that don't. Remove the clams from their shells, or leave on the half-shell. Set aside both the clams and their stock to cool.

2. Fry the pork or bacon in the oil until crisp. Remove with a slotted spoon and reserve. Add the onion and garlic and cook until translucent. Add a sprinkling of black pepper, the thyme, potatoes, clam stock, and the pork or bacon. Cook until the potatoes are just cooked.

3. Add the milk and cream and bring to a boil. Cook for a further 2–3 minutes, then add the clams and allow them to heat through. Check the seasoning, sprinkle with the parsley and serve with hot crusty bread or in the traditional way with crackers.

PIGS IN A BLANKET

These are particularly popular with children, who may enjoy making them themselves, providing they are well supervised

Makes 16

INGREDIENTS:

1 8-oz can croissant dough or ready-made flaky pastry
Dijon mustard
16 cocktail frankfurters
1 egg
1 tbsp milk

PREPARATION:

1. Preheat the oven to 350F.

2. Unroll the dough and separate it into four rectangles. Divide each rectangle into 3-inch-long strips. Spread each strip with a thin coating of mustard, then wrap each frank up in it, placing the rolls a few inches apart on a lightly oiled cookie sheet, seam sides down.

3. Beat the egg and milk together and brush the outsides of the rolls with the mixture. Bake for about 15 minutes or until the rolls are puffy and golden. Serve warm.

BARBECUE WINGS

An Indonesian-style satay, made with chopped scallions and red peppers, crushed garlic, peanut butter and a little curry powder would make a good dipping sauce for plain barbecued or fried chicken wings. Or a blue cheese sauce accompanied by sticks of celery would be nice. This dry rub adds a delicious taste to wings and will retain its flavor for a few weeks if kept in an airtight container and a dry, cool place.

Serves 4–6

INGREDIENTS:

4 tbsp coriander seeds
4 tbsp cumin seeds
4 tbsp curry powder
4 tbsp ground ginger
2 tbsp allspice
1 tbsp each ground black and red pepper
12 or more chicken wings

PREPARATION:

1. Gently toast the coriander and cumin seeds in a dry skillet, allow to cool, then grind in a blender or pound using a pestle and mortar. Mix with the curry powder, ginger, allspice and the two peppers.

2. Cut each chicken wing into two pieces, discarding the tips. Coat the wings thoroughly in the spice mixture, shaking off the excess before transferring them to a hot barbecue. Alternatively, the wings can be deep-fried at 350F until lightly browned.

NACHOS WITH CREAMY AVOCADO (overleaf)

Nachos were apparently invented by Ignacio Anaya at the Victory Club restaurant in the Mexican border town of Piedras Negras, and were simply fried tortilla chips topped with cheese and jalapeños. This is a slight variation on the original theme, but do be careful when using other types of chilis as there are huge differences in the amount of heat they produce. Serve with Mexican beers or margaritas.

Serves 4

INGREDIENTS:
8 oz guacamole (avocado) dip
1 clove of garlic, crushed
1 tsp taco seasoning
Dash of Tabasco sauce
1 cup mozzarella cheese, diced
1 ripe avocado, chopped
5 oz tortilla chips
2 sliced jalapeño chilies (pickled or bottled)
1 cup Cheddar cheese, grated
3 tbsp sour cream
2 tomatoes, quartered
2 tbsp snipped chives

PREPARATION:
1. Preheat the broiler to hot. Mix together the first four ingredients, then stir in the mozzarella and the avocado, adding more Tabasco if necessary.

2. Arrange the nachos around the edge of a heatproof plate and sprinkle the chilies and Cheddar cheese over them. Place under the broiler for 2–3 minutes until the cheese melts.

3. Spoon the avocado mixture into the center, spoon the sour cream over that, and garnish with tomatoes and chives.

BLACK BEAN SALSA

This is a quickly prepared no-fat, no-cook dip to serve with nachos.

Makes a generous cupful

INGREDIENTS:
15 oz canned black beans
6 tbsp ready-made pico de gallo (hot salsa)
1 tbsp fresh lime juice
1 clove of garlic, crushed

Garnish:
Cilantro, chopped
Diced tomatoes
Thinly sliced peppers

PREPARATION:
1. Thoroughly rinse and drain the beans, then place them with the other ingredients in a blender and process until smooth.

2. Garnish with cilantro, diced tomatoes and thinly sliced red peppers.

CHICKEN NOODLE SOUP

So comforting and nourishing is this classic soup that it has been claimed as a universal panacea, a cure for everything. Thin shreds of chicken can be added to the soup after it has been strained and before serving.

Serves 4

INGREDIENTS:
4–5 lb chicken pieces or 1 whole chicken
1 small onion, quartered
2 carrots, peeled and chopped
2 sticks of celery, chopped
Salt and black pepper
2 oz vermicelli or capellini
1–2 tbsp chopped flat-leaf parsley

PREPARATION:
1. Place the chicken, onion, carrot and celery in a large pan with a lid. Fill with water to cover the chicken, bring to a boil, then immediately turn the heat down to a very gentle bubble.

2. Simmer for about 1 hour until the liquid has reduced by half, skimming off the scum with a large spoon as it comes to the surface (this will help give a good clear stock).

3. Pass the liquid through cheesecloth or a very fine sieve into a smaller pan or bowl and leave to cool. Refrigerate, and preferably the next day remove any fat and sediment which has set on top.

4. Bring the soup gently back to a boil, season well, then add the pasta, cooking for 2 or 3 minutes until tender. Serve the soup piping hot, sprinkled with parsley.

FISH

NEW ORLEANS FISH CREOLE (opposite)
For a special occasion, replace the white fish with large shrimp but reduce the cooking time.

Serves 4

INGREDIENTS:
2 tbsp butter
1 large onion, chopped
1 clove of garlic, crushed
2 sticks of celery, chopped
14 oz canned chopped tomatoes
Salt and pepper
1 tsp curry powder
1 tsp Worcestershire sauce
1/2 tsp Tabasco sauce
8 plaice or lemon sole fillets, rolled and secured with
 cocktail sticks
1¼ cups American long-grain rice
2½ cups fish stock

GARNISH:
1 green pepper, seeded and thinly sliced
Orange slices
Fresh basil leaves

PREPARATION:
1. Heat the butter in a skillet, add the onion, garlic and celery and cook for 5–7 minutes until soft. Stir in the tomatoes, the seasonings, the curry powder and the two sauces, and bring to a boil.

2. Place the fish on top of the sauce and simmer gently, covered, steaming the fish for 10–15 minutes until it is tender. Remove the fish and keep it warm.

3. Cook the sauce for a further 10 minutes until it has thickened.

4. Meanwhile, place the rice in the stock, bring to a boil, then simmer, covered, for 12–15 minutes until tender and the liquid has been absorbed.

5. Place the rice on a serving dish, arrange the fish on top, then pour the sauce over it. Serve garnished with the green pepper, orange slices and basil.

LOBSTER NEWBURG
When lobsters are as delicious as they are in New

England they need little more than a good mayonnaise. However, this is a classic American way of serving lobster hot.

Serves 4

INGREDIENTS:
2 good-sized lobsters, cooked and cooled
6 tbsp butter
4–5 tbsp Madeira or dry sherry
1¼ cups heavy cream
4 large egg yolks
Cooked rice
1/2 tsp salt
1/4 tsp cayenne pepper
2 tsp lemon juice

GARNISH:
Paprika
Sprigs of chervil

PREPARATION:
1. Remove the legs and claws from the lobsters. Crack the claws and remove all the flesh.

2. Cut away and discard the heads, then place the bodies flat and cut them into two lengthways through the middle. Remove the flesh and cut it into bite-sized pieces. Place in a bowl with the flesh from the claws.

3. In a pan, melt the butter until bubbling, then add the lobster and cook it for about 1 minute. Pour in the Madeira and half the cream and simmer very gently for about 2 minutes.

4. Beat the egg yolks with the rest of the cream. Whisk in 3–4 tablespoons of the hot Madeira cream mixture, then immediately pour all the egg mixture into the hot cream pan, stirring constantly. Cook gently over a moderate heat until the sauce thickens, but on no account let it boil.

5. Scrub out the lobster shells and dry them well. Arrange them on serving plates and fill with the hot cooked rice.

6. Season the lobster and its sauce to taste with the salt, cayenne and lemon juice and serve immediately in the rice-filled shells, sprinkled with paprika and sprigs of chervil.

HANGTOWN FRY

Even though this was supposedly a condemned man's last meal, it is nevertheless an excellent way of serving oysters, especially to those who can't face eating them raw. Try them for a very special brunch.

Serves 4

INGREDIENTS:
12 oysters
4 large eggs
1 cup crushed crackers
1 tbsp all-purpose flour
Salt and chili pepper
2 tbsp butter or oil

2 tbsp heavy cream
1 tbsp chopped fresh parsley
1 tbsp fresh grated Parmesan cheese
Lemon juice
4 slices bacon, crisply broiled

PREPARATION:
1. Shuck the oysters and strain their juice into a small bowl. Add 3 eggs and and a pinch of salt and beat lightly to break the eggs up.

2. Place the crushed crackers on a small plate, a lightly-beaten egg on another and the flour, lightly seasoned with salt and chili pepper, on yet another. First dip the oysters in flour, then in the egg, then in the cracker crumbs, so that they are well-coated.

14

3. Heat half the butter in a small non-stick pan and fry the oysters until crisply golden. Remove and keep warm.

4. Clean the pan, if necessary, then add the rest of the butter and swirl in the cream, half the parsley, the beaten eggs with the oyster juice, Parmesan cheese and seasoning. Mix well and heat gently, adding the oysters to the pan at the last minute.

5. Add a squeeze of lemon juice, sprinkle with the rest of the parsley, and serve with the bacon.

BLACKENED FISH STEAKS (left)

This is a fast and fierce way of cooking firm fish. It was made so popular by Paul Prudhomme during the 1980s that it has become one of the classics of Creole cooking. The fish should be only slightly charred on the outside but still succulent in the middle. It should not resemble burnt toast!

Serves 3

INGREDIENTS:

2 tsp paprika
1 1/2 tsp salt
1/2 tsp each onion powder, garlic powder, white
 pepper, black pepper, dried dill and dried oregano
3 thick fish steaks, e.g. catfish, codfish, salmon, shark,
 swordfish or tuna
6 tbsp butter
Lemon wedges to garnish

PREPARATION:

1. Mix all 8 seasonings together, then dip the fish steaks into the mixture to coat them well.

2. Heat half the butter in a large skillet until it is on the point of turning brown. Add the steaks and cook them on each side, taking their thickness into account, until they are only just cooked through.

3. Transfer them immediately to an ovenproof dish and keep warm. Add the rest of the butter to the pan and heat it until it sizzles, then spoon the seasoned butter quickly over the fish. Serve with lemon wedges and plenty of fresh bread.

SWINGIN' LOUISIANA GUMBO (right)

A gumbo lies somewhere between a thick soup and a thin stew. The name is thought to have originated in the French-based patois spoken by some African-Americans and Creoles in Louisiana. Okra is considered the essential ingredient, as it adds a rich and luscious quality to the stew. If fresh oysters are not available, use clams, scallops, or even mussels.

Serves 4–6

INGREDIENTS:

12 oysters in their shells
2 tbsp butter
2 medium onions, finely chopped
1 1/2 tbsp flour
14 oz canned tomatoes
10 oz okra, cut into 1/2-inch pieces
5 cups fish stock
2 cloves of garlic, crushed
2 tsp salt
2 tsp Worcestershire sauce
1 tsp hot pepper sauce
1 1/4 cups American long-grain rice
1 lb large shrimp, peeled and deveined
8 oz fresh crabmeat

PREPARATION:

1. Carefully open the oysters, reserving their juice, and refrigerate them until required.

2. Melt the butter in a large heavy-based saucepan and cook the onion for 10 minutes over a low heat, stirring from time to time. Add the flour and cook for 2 minutes, stirring all the while.

3. Stir in the tomatoes and okra, bring to a boil, and cook for 5 minutes until the mixture thickens slightly.

4. Add the juice from the oysters and the fish stock to the okra pan. Stir in the garlic, salt, Worcestershire sauce and hot pepper sauce. Bring to a boil, cover with a lid, and cook over a low heat for 1 hour, stirring occasionally.

5. Meanwhile, cook the rice in boiling salted water for 12–15 minutes until tender. Drain and set aside.

6. Add the oysters, shrimp and crabmeat to the pan with the stock and seasonings and cook for a further 5 minutes until tender.

7. Stir the cooked rice into the pan and heat through. Serve immediately

SHRIMP IN GARLIC BUTTER

Shrimp is America's favorite seafood and no wonder; it is delicious, versatile, easy to cook and a valuable source of protein. However, you will find that most shrimp has been frozen and this often applies to so-called fresh shrimp as well. This is no problem as it freezes very successfully.

Serves 4–5

INGREDIENTS:
1 lb raw shrimp, deveined
1/2 cup butter, melted
3 cloves of garlic, crushed
2 tbsp chopped fresh parsley
2–3 tbsp lemon juice
Salt and black pepper
2 tbsp chopped parsley

PREPARATION:

1. Rinse and dry the shrimp. Have ready a large sheet of aluminum foil to make a parcel.

2. Mix together the remaining ingredients, stir in the shrimp, then tip them onto the foil, folding it up to make a leakproof parcel.

3. Place on a barbecue for 10–15 minutes, or less, depending on how hot it is, shaking the parcel occasionally so that the shrimp become coated in the garlic butter.

4. Serve immediately with hot crusty bread to mop up the juice.

MARYLAND CRAB CAKES (right)

East Coast crabs are some of the very best and quite different from the small Blue Crab of the south or the Alaskan King Crab with its long and meaty legs full of firm, white flesh. Avoid adding unnecessary flavors and serve the crab cakes either with a light salsa or fresh chili sauce, or simply with a good mayonnaise.

Makes 10

INGREDIENTS:
1 lb fresh white crabmeat
Salt and black pepper
1 tsp anchovy essence or a few drops chili sauce
Good squeeze of lemon juice
1 tsp mustard
1 small egg (separated)
1 tbsp each finely chopped chives and parsley
1/2 cup flour, sieved
2 tbsp butter
2 tbsp oil

PREPARATION:

1. Flake the crabmeat, then mix it with the seasonings, anchovy essence, lemon juice, mustard, egg white and herbs and chill well.

2. In a shallow dish, lightly beat the egg yolk with 1 tablespoon of water. Place the flour in another shallow dish. Divide the mixture into 10 small neat cakes, dip them into the flour and then the egg, draining off the excess.

3. Heat half the butter and oil in a skillet until it bubbles, then cook half the crab cakes, basting and turning them frequently until golden (about 6–7 minutes altogether). Transfer to paper towels to drain while you cook the rest in the remainder of the butter and oil. Serve hot.

MEAT

HASH

This favorite supper dish is made with leftover cooked brisket or salt beef and cooked beets so that it becomes a rich red color. It can be enlivened with Worcestershire or Tabasco sauce and is often served topped with fried or poached eggs.

Serves 4

INGREDIENTS:
1 tbsp sunflower oil
1 clove of garlic, chopped
4-oz piece of bacon, chopped
1 small onion, chopped
3 cups cooked corned beef brisket, chopped
2–3 cooked and peeled beets, diced
3 cups cooked potatoes, chopped
2 tbsp chopped fresh parsley
3–4 tbsp heavy cream
Salt and black pepper

PREPARATION:
1. Heat the oil in a large skillet and fry the garlic, bacon and onion until tender and slightly golden. Drain off the excess fat.

2. Add the beef, beets and potatoes and turn the mixture gently over a medium heat until it begins to crisp at the edges.

3. Stir in the parsley, cream, and seasoning to taste, then spread the mixture out evenly. Reduce the heat and leave to cook gently for about 30 minutes. (If excess fat rises to the surface it can be removed with a large spoon.)

4. The hash is ready when a golden crust forms on the underside. It can now be served straight from the pan or transferred carefully onto a serving dish.

COLLARD GREENS WITH SMOKED BACON

These flat, blue-green leaves taste not unlike kale or turnip greens, and like them are members of the mustard family. Depending on their age they can be mild and tender or have a slightly hotter flavor. But slowly cooked with pork or bacon, and perhaps a touch of chili, the result is quite delicious.

Serves 4

INGREDIENTS:
2-lb piece of smoked bacon, preferably the knuckle end
2 lb collard greens, kale or chard (or a mixture of all three)
1 tsp sugar
$1/2$–1 tsp chili sauce or dried chili flakes

PREPARATION:
1. Place the bacon in a large pan and cover it with water. Bring to a boil and simmer for 1 hour, removing any scum that rises to the surface.

2. Wash the greens well and remove the thick, tough stalks. Then tear them into even-sized strips and add to the pan of bacon along with the sugar and chilli. Cover and cook for a further 30 minutes or longer, until the bacon and the greens are tender.

3. Check the level of the water in the pan in case it dries out completely, but you actually want most of the liquid to cook away, leaving a richly-flavored gravy. Serve with Hoppin' John (page 36) or Boston Baked Beans (page 39) for an economical and tasty supper.

TEXAS CHILI (right)

Texas is the true home of chili con carne, where it is traditionally served with home-cooked beans, locally-grown rice, sour cream, guacamole, chopped scallions and tomatoes, corn chips and many other condiments.

Serves 4–6

INGREDIENTS:
2 tbsp sunflower oil
2 lb chuck steak, trimmed and cubed
2 large onions, sliced
4 cloves of garlic, crushed
6 jalapeño chilies, seeded and chopped
2 tsp cumin
2 tsp chili powder
Salt
2 tsp dried oregano
$1^3/4$ lb canned chopped tomatoes
1 can red kidney beans (optional)
Cooked rice

PREPARATION:

1. Heat the oil in a large pan and brown the meat in small batches.

2. Add the onion and garlic and cook for 5 minutes to soften them.

3. Stir in the chilies, cumin and chili powder. Cook over a medium heat for 2–3 minutes. Season with salt, add the oregano and tomatoes, bring to a boil and simmer, covered, for 1¼ –1½ hours until the meat is tender. If using, drain the red kidney beans and rinse

them in fresh water. Add them at the end of the cooking time, heating them through in the chili.

4. Adjust the seasoning to taste and serve with rice, plus sour cream and other accompaniments.

JAMBALAYA (overleaf)
This is a true Cajun dish from the heart of Louisiana and a perfect way of transforming leftovers into a hearty family meal.

Serves 4

INGREDIENTS:
2 tbsp vegetable oil
1 large onion, chopped
3 sticks of celery, chopped
1 green pepper, seeded and chopped
2 cloves of garlic, crushed
8 oz andouille or similar sausage, sliced
2 1/2 cups chicken stock

1 1/4 cups American long-grain rice
1/2 tsp cayenne pepper
2 large tomatoes, skinned and chopped
8 oz cooked shrimp, peeled
8 oz cooked chicken, chopped

PREPARATION:
1. Heat the oil in a large pan and add the onion,

celery, pepper and garlic. Cover with a lid and cook over a low heat for 10–15 minutes until soft.

2. Add the sausage and cook for 2 minutes. Stir in the stock, rice, cayenne and tomatoes. Bring to a boil, cover with a lid, and simmer for 12–15 minutes until the rice is tender and the stock has been absorbed.

3. Stir in the shrimp and chicken and cook very gently until the chicken is thoroughly heated through.

4. Spoon the jambalaya into a large dish and serve immediately.

KANSAS-STYLE RIBS WITH RICE (below)

Kansas City considers itself the barbecue capital of the world, but these ribs would taste good just about anywhere.

Serves 4–6

INGREDIENTS:
3-lb side of pork spareribs
1¼ cups American long-grain rice
5 cups vegetable stock

DRY RUB:
1 tbsp cumin
1 tbsp black pepper
2 tsp chili powder
1 tsp salt
2 tbsp paprika
2 tbsp dark brown sugar

WET SAUCE:
1 cup white wine vinegar
1 tbsp hot pepper sauce
1 tbsp dark brown sugar
1½ tsp black pepper
½ tsp salt

PREPARATION:

1. Preheat the oven to 350F.

2. Trim any excess fat from the ribs. Mix together the ingredients for the dry rub, then apply it to the surface of the meat, rubbing it well in.

3. Put the ribs into a roasting pan and bake them for 1½ hours. Remove from the oven. Mix together the ingredients for the wet sauce, brush this over the ribs and set them aside.

4. Cook the rice in the stock, covered, for 12–15 minutes until the rice is tender and has absorbed all the stock.

5. Meanwhile, preheat the broiler or make sure an outdoor barbecue is hot. Cook the ribs for a further 10–15 minutes, basting and turning them occasionally.

6. Spoon the rice into a serving dish, cut up the ribs, and pile them on top of the rice. Serve with A Mean Barbecue Sauce, page 28.

PORK WITH HOT BEAN SAUCE (opposite)

Chinese take out is popular all over the country, and as specialty ingredients become easier to find, more people are stirring it up at home.

Serves 4

INGREDIENTS:
1 tbsp sunflower oil
2 cloves of garlic, crushed
1¼ lb pork tenderloin, cut into cubes
½ jar black bean sauce
⅔ cup coconut milk
1 tsp finely chopped or shredded chili
2 tbsp dry sherry
Soy sauce
Jasmine or basmati rice, cooked
Cilantro, chopped

PREPARATION:

1. Heat the oil and garlic in a wok or small frying pan until a haze appears on the surface of the oil. Remove the garlic before it burns and discard, then add the pork.

2. Stir-fry the pork briskly until well sealed, then reduce the heat and pour off the excess fat.

3. Stir in the sauce, coconut milk, chili and sherry and cook over a moderate heat until the sauce thickens and the pork is tender. Add soy sauce to taste.

4. Serve with rice and sprinkle with cilantro.

CHINESE CHICKEN AND VEGETABLE STIR-FRY

Stir-frying is very quick and healthy as only a little oil needs to be used; but it must be done quickly and over a very high heat. A wok is not essential but it does add a greater surface area over which to spread the food. The secret is to prepare everything beforehand, cutting meat and vegetables into even, bite-sized pieces.

Serves 4

INGREDIENTS:
1 lb chicken fillets
2 tbsp sunflower oil
6 oz carrots, peeled and cut into sticks
1 red pepper, seeded and sliced
4 oz sugar snap or snow peas, trimmed
4 oz baby corn
5 oz pineapple chunks
4 oz bean sprouts
Scant 2 cups sweet and sour or tomato and mushroom
  sauce
1 tbsp clear honey
1 tbsp dry sherry
1 tbsp white wine
2 tbsp light soy sauce
Egg noodles, cooked

PREPARATION:

1. Cut the chicken into thin strips. Heat the oil in a large wok or skillet and stir-fry the chicken over a high heat until golden and almost cooked through.

2. Add the carrot, pepper, peas and corn and cook for 5 minutes, tossing while stir-frying. Then add in the remaining ingredients.

3. Continue stir-frying over a high heat for a further 2–3 minutes (the vegetables should remain crisp). Serve immediately with freshly cooked noodles.

JERK PORK

This spicy Caribbean treatment of pork is now a popular barbecue dish everywhere. It evolved as a way of

preserving meat for several weeks and will certainly add to your barbecue selection!

Serves 4

INGREDIENTS:
2 tbsp dark soy sauce
2 tbsp tomato ketchup
Freshly grated rind of 1 lime
2 tbsp fresh lime juice
2 tbsp dark brown sugar
1 tsp mixed spice
1 tsp chili powder
1 tsp paprika
$1/2$ tsp ground black pepper
$1/2$ tsp ground cinnamon
2 tsp chopped fresh garlic
1 tsp salt
$1^1/2$ lb pork steaks, or boneless chops

PREPARATION:
1. Mix the seasonings and all the other ingredients to a thick paste. Brush the pork all over with the paste and set it aside to absorb the flavors for up to 1 hour.

2. Barbecue or broil the pork for 2–3 minutes each side until the pork is tender and begins to blacken. Serve with hot fresh rolls, focaccia, chapatis or other specialty breads.

BEEF STEW WITH DUMPLINGS (right)
An excellent family meal that can be prepared a day or two ahead to allow the flavors to mature. For a livelier flavor, add more fresh diced vegetables and herbs towards the end of cooking and before adding the dumplings.

Serves 4

INGREDIENTS:
1 tbsp beef dripping or oil
8 oz button onions, peeled
$1^1/2$ lb boneless stewing beef, cut into cubes
2 tbsp flour
$3^3/4$ cups beef stock
Salt and freshly ground black pepper
1 clove of garlic, crushed
2 sticks of celery, chopped
1 cup each chopped carrots and turnips
1 cup ripe tomatoes, peeled and chopped

DUMPLINGS:
1 cup all-purpose flour
Good pinch of salt
2 tsp baking powder
2 tbsp chopped mixed fresh herbs
4 tbsp frozen butter, grated

PREPARATION:
1. Heat the fat or oil in a large saucepan and fry the onions until lightly browned. Transfer them to a plate using a slotted spoon. Fry the meat, a few pieces at a time, until brown all over, then remove.

2. Blend the flour into the remaining juices and stir with a wooden spoon until a rich brown color develops. Remove from the heat and, stirring constantly, gradually add the stock, allowing it to return to a boil and thicken.

3. Add the seasoning and garlic, vegetables, the button onions and the meat. Bring back to a boil, cover, and simmer for about $1^1/2$ hours.

4. Meanwhile, prepare the dumplings by mixing the flour, salt, baking powder, herbs and grated butter together, adding sufficient cold water to make a soft dough. With wetted hands, form into 10–12 small dumplings, which will swell on cooking.

5. Remove the lid of the saucepan, check the seasonings, and add the dumplings. Bring back to a boil and allow the liquid to gently simmer while the dumplings cook. If the liquid reduces too much, add a little extra hot water and continue to cook until the dumplings have nearly doubled their size.

SPICY SOUTHERN FRIED CHICKEN (overleaf)
This famous dish is hard to beat, so make plenty of the seasoning mix and store it away ready to use when the need arises. Use vegetable shortening instead of oil for a much crisper result and drain the chicken well on a rack.

Serves 4

INGREDIENTS:
8–10 small chicken portions
1 egg
3 tbsp water
Oil for deep frying

SEASONING MIX:

1 tbsp paprika
1 tbsp celery salt
1 tbsp onion powder
1 tbsp mustard powder
1 tsp red pepper
Salt and freshly ground black pepper
1 tbsp flour

PREPARATION:

1. Wash the chicken portions and dry them carefully on paper towels. Place on a large tray.

2. Mix all the seasonings together, adding plenty of salt and black pepper, and finally the flour.

3. In a shallow bowl, thoroughly beat the egg with the water. Dip the chicken portions into the egg, then into the seasoning mix, coating them thoroughly. Return them to the tray and leave them in the refrigerator to firm up slightly.

4. Meanwhile, heat the oil in a deep-fryer to 350F. Fry the chicken in batches, turning the portions carefully once or twice until evenly browned all over. (They will need 6–8 minutes, but make sure they are well cooked through.) If they appear to be browning too quickly, slightly reduce the heat in the fryer, if necessary removing the chicken from the fat while it cools down.

5. Drain the portions on a rack and serve with potato salad and a green salad or fries.

BBQ CHICKEN WITH CHILI GLAZE (above)
Fresh chilies add a spicy flavor as well as a hot kick and are wonderful as part of a sweet-sour combination. Omit if you prefer, but you could use just a little (half a teaspoon) rather than leave them out altogether.

Serves 4

INGREDIENTS:
4 chicken portions
2 tbsp maple syrup
1 tsp Worcestershire sauce
1 tbsp olive oil
1 clove of garlic, crushed
1 tsp chopped fresh red chili
Salt and black pepper

PREPARATION:
1. Clean and wipe dry the chicken portions, leaving the skin on as a protection against the heat of the barbecue. Place in a shallow dish.

2. Mix together the remaining ingredients, spread evenly over the chicken, then leave in a cool place for 1–2 hours. Turn the chicken and rub the marinade in once more during this time.

3. Cook over a barbecue or under a hot broiler for at least 20 minutes, turning every 5 minutes to ensure even cooking. Make sure that the chicken is thoroughly cooked and that the juices run clear with no pink tinge.

A MEAN BARBECUE SAUCE

A good barbecue sauce is a must for steak, ribs, hamburgers, chicken pieces or chunks of fish. This one is ideal as a dip or can be used to coat food before cooking. But beware! It is loaded with chilis and not for the faint-hearted.

Makes about 6½ cups

INGREDIENTS:
5 tbsp sunflower or olive oil
1 onion, chopped
2–3 cloves of garlic, crushed
4 plum tomatoes, peeled, seeded and chopped
1 large sweet red pepper, seeded and finely chopped
1–2 hot red chilis, seeded and finely diced (see Tip below)
1¾ lb canned chopped tomatoes
1–2 tsp light brown sugar
½ tsp dried oregano
Juice of 1 lime
Worcestershire sauce
Salt and black pepper

PREPARATION:
1. Heat the oil in a saucepan and add the onion, garlic, fresh tomatoes and red pepper. Cook gently for about 5 minutes until the vegetables are soft but not brown.

2. Add the remaining ingredients and simmer for a further 30 minutes or until reduced to the thickness you require. If you prefer a smooth sauce, pass through a fine sieve or blend for a few seconds in a food processor. Check the seasoning.

3. Cool, then store for no more than a week in a jar in the fridge. Use as required.

Tip: Treat chilis with respect. Use rubber gloves when preparing them and refrain from touching eyes or other sensitive areas until you have very thoroughly washed your hands. Remember that the seeds are the hottest part of the chili, so discarding them will give a slightly milder result.

DAD'S HOMEMADE HAMBURGERS (left)

The hamburger originated in the German city of Hamburg where it started life as a raw beef dish also containing onions, capers and anchovies (steak tartare). However, someone got the idea of cooking the beef and the hamburger as we now know it was born. It is important to use good-quality lean beef with about 20 percent fat to ensure that the result is tender and delectable.

Serve 4

INGREDIENTS:

1 lb ground chuck
1 cup fresh breadcrumbs
4 tbsp milk
1 small onion, finely grated
1/2 tsp mustard

Salt and pepper
2 tbsp vegetable oil
2 tbsp butter
8 burger buns
Lettuce leaves

PREPARATION:

1. Combine the beef, breadcrumbs, milk, onion, mustard and seasoning together, then divide equally into eight. Shape into 1/2-inch-thick burgers.

2. Heat the oil and butter in a large skillet and over a high heat fry four burgers at a time for 1 minute on each side.

3. Reduce the heat and cook for 6–8 minutes, turning occasionally. Keep warm while frying the others. Serve in buns lined with lettuce leaves and accompanied by piccalilli, green tomato or other relishes. Thin slices of Cheddar or blue cheese could also be added, placed on top or between two hamburgers.

SANDWICH VARIATIONS (left)

There are any number of alternative fillings you could try as a change from the traditional burger, so why not let your imagination run riot! Here are just four suggestions.

Serves 1

1. TURKEY AND SWEETCORN

INGREDIENTS:

Slice of cooked turkey leg, chopped
1 tbsp drained sweetcorn kernels
1 tbsp mayonnaise
Salt and pepper
Shredded lettuce

PREPARATION:

Mix the turkey, sweetcorn, mayonnaise and seasoning together. Spread on one half of a buttered bun, top with lettuce and the other half of the bun.

2. HAM AND CHEESE

INGREDIENTS:

2 thin slices Cheddar cheese or cheese slices
1 or two slices of ham

MEAT

PREPARATION:
Split a bun and lightly toast each half. Place a slice of cheese on the bun, top with the ham, then the other slice of cheese and broil until the cheese melts. Top with the other half of the bun.

3. FISHBURGER

INGREDIENTS:
1 boneless fish steak or fillet
1 egg, beaten
1/2 cup fresh breadcrumbs
1 tbsp thick mayonnaise
Shredded romaine or lollo rosso lettuce
1 tbsp tomato relish

PREPARATION:
Egg and breadcrumb the fish and fry in a little oil until crisp on both sides. Spread the base of a split, warmed bun with mayonnaise, then lettuce, then the fish, and top with relish to taste.

4. BACON FRY-UP

INGREDIENTS:
1 tbsp oil
1/2 small onion, cut into rings
2 slices of bacon, rinds removed and roughly chopped up
Arugula or baby spinach leaves
Squeeze of lemon juice

PREPARATION:
Heat the oil in a very small pan. Fry the onion and bacon over a medium heat until the onion is tender and the bacon slightly crisp. Arrange in a warmed bun with the salad leaves, dressed with a little lemon juice.

THANKSGIVING TURKEY WITH PECAN STUFFING
(above right)
Turkey is the first choice for Thanksgiving or when a large crowd of friends and relations needs to be fed, and a delicious stuffing makes it even more special. Turkey makes a great sandwich or po' boy filling in the remote event of there being leftovers.

Serves 10–12

INGREDIENTS:
14-lb fresh turkey, with giblets

4 oz fat bacon, sliced
6 tbsp butter
1 large onion, roughly chopped
2/3 cup dry white wine

PECAN STUFFING:
3/4 cup pecans, chopped
1 cup fresh breadcrumbs
2 tbsp butter, softened
1 onion, finely chopped
1 egg, beaten
Salt and pepper
Parsley sprigs to garnish

PREPARATION:
1. Rinse the turkey and dry it well. Lay the bacon over the breast, securing it with cocktail sticks. Preheat the oven to 325F.

2. Combine the ingredients for the stuffing and mix well.

3. Put the stuffing into the cavity of the turkey and secure with a skewer, then rub the butter into the surface of the bird. Put it into a roasting pan and insert a meat thermometer between the breast and thigh, ensuring that it does not touch the bone.

4. Cover the turkey loosely with aluminum foil and roast it in the oven for 4 hours, basting occasionally.

5. Meanwhile, put the giblets and onion into a small saucepan, cover with water, bring to a boil, cover, then simmer for 1 hour. Strain the liquid and reserve it for the gravy.

6. The turkey is cooked when the temperature shows 350F on the thermometer. Remove to a warm serving dish and leave to rest for 20 minutes.

7. Place the roasting pan over a gentle heat and stir with a wooden spoon to loosen the sediment, then gradually add the giblet stock and the wine. Bring to a boil and simmer for 10 minutes, stirring occasionally. Adjust the seasoning to taste.

8. Remove the bacon, cocktail sticks and skewer from the turkey, and serve, garnished with the parsley.

PORK TENDERLOIN WITH PEPPER VODKA AND CRANBERRIES (below)

Nowadays, pork is bred to be leaner and more tender than it used to be, when it was regarded as a fatty meat. This was why it was usually served with fruit to help counteract the richness. Fruit with pork continues to be popular and cranberries, with their intense flavor and delicious tartness, are especially good with pork, as is a little alcohol!

Serves 2

INGREDIENTS:
10 oz pork tenderloin
2 tsp Dijon mustard
6 slices from a white French loaf
Olive oil
3 tbsp pepper vodka
1/2 tsp black peppercorns
6 large unpeeled cloves of garlic
2 tbsp cranberry sauce
2 tsp finely chopped onion
4–5 tbsp butter
2/3 cup red wine

PREPARATION:
1. Trim the tenderloin of all fat and membranes and cut it into two equal pieces. Spread with the mustard, cover, then leave at room temperature for 2 hours or overnight in the refrigerator.

2. Preheat the oven to 325F. Make some croutons by spreading the bread slices (which should be as thick as a finger) with the oil and baking them until crisp. While still warm, sprinkle them with half the pepper vodka.

3. Roast the peppercorns in a heavy-based pan until they pop and give off a pleasant aroma. Crush roughly when cool.

4. Increase the oven temperature to 425F. Boil the unpeeled garlic cloves in a little water until soft, then crush them with a fork and pass them through a fine sieve to remove the tough skins. Spread half the garlic directly onto the croutons, then mix the remainder into the cranberry sauce with half the crushed peppercorns, keeping the cranberries as whole as possible. Spread on top of the garlic on the croutons.

5. Put the chopped onion and the rest of the crushed, roasted peppercorns into a small roasting pan and add the two pieces of tenderloin, dotted with a tablespoon of butter. Roast for 12–15 minutes until just cooked through, when the juices should run clear. Remove the meat, cover, and leave to rest. Put the croutons back in the oven to heat through and to lightly brown the edges.

6. Place the roasting pan over a gentle heat and pour in the red wine. Reduce until only 2 or 3 tablespoons

of liquid are left. Stir in the remainder of the pepper vodka, then remove from the heat and whisk in as much of the remaining butter as needed to thicken the sauce (you may need a little more).

7. Serve the pork sliced with a little of the sauce and accompanied by the croutons.

ALL-AMERICAN MEATLOAF (above)

What could be better than a tasty meatloaf, the faithful standby of all home cooks. It should be firm but juicy and is traditionally served with mashed potatoes. However, a robust tomato or barbecue sauce would not go amiss.

Serves 4–6

INGREDIENTS:

2 lb ground beef chuck (or beef, veal and pork mixed)
1 medium onion, minced
1 tbsp Worcestershire sauce
5–6 tbsp tomato ketchup
1 tsp salt
1/2 tsp black pepper
2 eggs
2 slices white bread, crusts removed
1/2 cup milk
2 tsp grain (Meaux) mustard
2 tbsp light brown sugar

PREPARATION:

1. Preheat the oven to 375F. In a large bowl, mix together the meat, onion, Worcestershire sauce, half

the ketchup, salt, pepper and the eggs.

2. In a small bowl, soak the bread in the milk for several minutes. Crumble the bread, then work it into the meat mixture. Lightly grease a loaf pan and fill it with the mixture, pressing it down lightly. Bake for 45 minutes.

3. While the meatloaf is in the oven, stir together the remaining ketchup, mustard and sugar. Brush evenly over the meatloaf and continue to cook until the meat is firm and has shrunk away from the sides of the pan. Check also that the juices run clear when a skewer is inserted in the middle of the meatloaf.

MEATBALLS WITH TOMATO SAUCE (below)

These make a great meal on their own, served with mashed potatoes or teamed with spaghetti.

Serves 4

INGREDIENTS:
TOMATO SAUCE:
6 tbsp olive oil
1 large onion, finely chopped
2 cloves of garlic, crushed
2 lb plum tomatoes, peeled, seeded and chopped
Salt and pepper
1 tsp sugar
2 bay leaves
1/4 cup fresh parsley, oregano, or basil, or a mixture of all three

MEATBALLS:
3/4 lb ground lean beef
1/2 cup breadcrumbs
2 tbsp Parmesan cheese, grated
1 small onion, very finely chopped or minced
1 clove of garlic, crushed
Rind of 1/2 lemon
1/4 cup fresh oregano or parsley, chopped
Pinch of nutmeg
1 egg, beaten
Salt and black pepper
Olive oil

PREPARATION:
1. Make the tomato sauce. Heat the oil in a large pan, add the onion, and fry until golden. Add the garlic and

cook gently for 1–2 minutes.

2. Add the tomatoes, seasoning, sugar and the herbs and simmer for 15–20 minutes until the sauce is slightly reduced. Remove the bay leaves.

3. Place the first ten ingredients for the meatballs into a large mixing bowl, season with salt and pepper, and mix thoroughly (use your hands for this). Divide the mixture into 12 and shape into even-sized balls.

4. Heat more olive oil in a large skillet and gently fry the meatballs until brown all over. Add the meatballs to the tomato sauce and simmer for 10 minutes.

Tip: As an alternative, a brown sauce can be made simply by adding a little flour to the pan residues after the meatballs have been fried. Add some beef stock, bring to a boil, and cook until the sauce is thick and smooth. Add a dash of cream before serving.

NEW ENGLAND BOILED DINNER (opposite)
This humble, hearty dish is a classic American favorite. Beets are occasionally added, which give a striking color to the finished dish. Any leftover beef could be used to make Hash (page 18).

Serves 6–8

INGREDIENTS:
4 lb brisket or corned beef
2 sticks of celery, chopped
Bay leaves
Pepper
4 large carrots, peeled and quartered
2 large onions, quartered
2 lb cabbage, cut into wedges

DUMPLINGS:
1 1/2 cups all-purpose flour
1 tsp baking powder
Pinch of salt
1 tsp mustard powder
1 tsp dried mixed herbs
4 tbsp butter

PREPARATION:
1. Place the beef in a large pan with the celery, a few bay leaves and the pepper. Cover with cold water and bring to a boil, removing any scum as it rises to the surface. Cover with a lid and simmer for 1 1/2 hours.

2. Add the carrots and onions, checking that there is sufficient water in the pan, and cook for a further 30 minutes or until the meat is tender.

3. To make the dumplings, sift the dry ingredients into a bowl, add the herbs and rub in the butter. Add sufficient cold water to form a soft dough and with floured hands shape into 12–16 dumplings.

4. Add the cabbage to the pan, then the dumplings, cover, and cook for a further 10–15 minutes.

5. To serve, transfer the meat to a warm serving dish and surround it with the vegetables and dumplings. Remove and drain the cabbage and serve it separately. Add a little slaked cornstarch to the juices and boil for a few minutes if you prefer a thicker gravy.

CORN DOGS
Frankfurters came to America along with German immigrants. However, this particular snack was invented by a Texan and has since traveled the length and breadth of America.

Serves 6

INGREDIENTS:
1/4 cup all-purpose flour
1/2 cup yellow cornmeal
Pinch of salt
Good pinch of baking soda
1/2 cup buttermilk
1/2 small egg, beaten
Vegetable oil
6 frankfurters
6 wooden sticks or skewers, well-soaked in water
Ketchup or mustard

PREPARATION:
1. Mix the first four ingredients together, then whisk in the buttermilk and the egg. When smooth, set aside for a few minutes.

2. Heat at least 2 inches of oil in a deep pan with a lid, or heat a deep-fat fryer with the correct amount of oil to about 350F.

3. Place each dog on a skewer, then coat well with the batter, draining off the excess. Cook three at a time until crisp and golden, then remove and drain. Serve hot with ketchup or mustard.

SALADS, SNACKS & SIDES

SUCCOTASH

Succotash comes from a Native American word meaning "boiled kernels of corn", which is an immediate clue to its main ingredient. It also combines lima, red kidney or other beans. This recipe has bacon added for flavor, but it would make a good, nourishing vegetarian dish if this was simply left out.

Serves 6

INGREDIENTS:
2 tbsp vegetable oil
1 lb lean smoked bacon hock, cubed
1 large onion, chopped
3 large cloves of garlic, finely chopped
1 red and 1 green pepper, seeded and sliced
1³/₄ lb canned lima beans, rinsed and drained
1³/₄ lb canned chick peas, rinsed and drained
1³/₄ lb canned sweetcorn, drained
1¹/₂ cups water
4 large firm tomatoes, seeded and roughly chopped
Seasoning to taste
1 cup Cheddar cheese, grated
Chopped parsley or cilantro

PREPARATION:
1. Heat the oil in a large pan and cook the chopped bacon over a high heat until slightly brown. Add the onion and garlic and continue cooking until they have softened but not colored.

2. Add the peppers, beans, chick peas and water and bring to a boil, then reduce the heat and simmer for 15 minutes. Add the tomatoes and sweetcorn and cook for a further 20 minutes or until the sauce has thickened and the bacon is tender.

3. Add seasoning to taste and serve sprinkled with a little cheese and chopped herb. Have a bowl of extra cheese at the table. Serve with cooked rice or fresh bread. If you are keeping the dish vegetarian, you could add a cup of heavy cream instead of or in addition to the cheese.

Tip: Should you decide to use fresh corn, cook 6 large cobs until almost tender. Let them cool until you can handle them comfortably then, cutting down with a sharp knife, separate the kernels from the cob. Add with the peppers, beans and chick peas (Step 2).

HASH BROWNS

These can be made using either cooked or raw potatoes, which some prefer as they keep their texture during cooking. Leftover potatoes can be used, smashed rather than mashed, and left unpeeled if preferred. Sometimes the potatoes are mixed with a little flour and formed into small cakes, rather like Polish latkes. This is not unlike the Swiss rösti.

Serves 4

INGREDIENTS:
1 lb potatoes, parboiled for 10 minutes
1 medium onion, finely chopped
2 cloves of garlic, crushed
Salt and pepper
5–6 tbsp each sunflower oil and butter

PREPARATION:
1. Peel the potatoes when cold and coarsely grate them into a large bowl. Add the onion, garlic and seasoning.

2. Heat half the oil and butter in a large skillet and add the potato mixture. Spread it out evenly and flatten it down with a spatula. Cook over a medium–high heat for 5–8 minutes until crisp underneath.

3. Carefully place a plate over the top (it should fit neatly just inside the pan rim) and flip the pan over so that the potatoes slip onto the plate.

4. Add the rest of the oil and butter to the pan, heat, then slide the potatoes back into the pan, uncooked side down. Continue cooking until golden and cooked through. Serve cut into wedges topped with a poached egg and broiled bacon, or as an accompaniment to steaks, grills or fried fish.

HOPPIN' JOHN (right)

This is a Carolina pilaf which arrived by a tortuous route, brought by Huguenots to America, who in turn had been introduced to pilafs by Muslims when they began to colonize Mediterranean Europe. Once in America, it was adopted by African Americans. This is a simplified method.

Serves 4

INGREDIENTS:

Generous 1/2 cup dried black-eyed peas
1 ham hock
1 large onion, chopped
Salt
1 1/4 cups American long-grain rice
1/2 tsp cayenne pepper
1/2 tsp black pepper
2 tbsp butter

PREPARATION:

1. Soak the peas and the ham overnight in enough water to cover.

2. Drain the peas and ham, put them into a large pan, pour 2 1/2 cups of water over them and bring to a boil. Cover with a lid and boil for 15 minutes.

3. Add the onion and simmer for 1 1/2–2 hours until the peas and ham are cooked.

37

4. Meanwhile, cook the rice in boiling salted water for 12–15 minutes until just tender.

5. Remove the ham from the pan of peas and remove the meat from the bone. Drain the peas and rice and mix them together with the meat. Stir in the cayenne pepper, black pepper and butter, heat through, and serve.

BOSTON BAKED BEANS

During their long cooking time, preferably on the day before you are going to eat them, the beans absorb all the wonderful flavors of the other ingredients and turn a rich, dark brown.

Serves 6–8

INGREDIENTS:

2¹/₂ cups small white kidney or navy beans
1 large onion, peeled and studded with 3 or 4 whole cloves
12-oz piece of salt pork with the rind left on
1 large onion, chopped
3 large cloves of garlic, minced
4 tbsp dark molasses
4 tbsp tomato ketchup
4 tbsp dark brown sugar
2 tbsp mild (Dijon) mustard
2 tsp minced or grated fresh ginger
1 tsp dried mixed herbs
1–2 tsp salt

PREPARATION:

1. Leave the beans to soak in water overnight, then drain and place them in a large pan with enough water to cover. Bring to a boil for 2 minutes, then remove from the heat, cover, and leave for 1 hour.

2. Drain the beans and return them to the pan with the onion and sufficient fresh water to cover. Bring to a boil and simmer until the beans are just tender.

3. Meanwhile, cut the pork into strips, place in a pan of cold water, bring to a boil, then simmer for 10 minutes. Drain, retaining the liquid.

4. In a small pan, fry the pork until the fat begins to run. Add the onion and garlic and cook gently for 1 minute without browning. Add the molasses, ketchup,

sugar, mustard and ginger. Mix well and cook gently until the onion is translucent. Preheat the oven to 350F.

5. In a Dutch oven or a heavy ovenproof casserole with a tight-fitting lid, layer the beans and the pork-molasses mix and sprinkle on the herbs. Slowly pour in 2¹/₂ cups of the bean liquid. Cover, and cook for 1¹/₂ hours.

6. Remove the lid, add salt, and continue cooking for another 1–1¹/₂ hours or until the beans are tender.

ROASTED SWEET POTATOES (opposite)

Candied sweet potatoes are a must with the Thanksgiving Turkey (page 30) and are often served with pork, duck and other roasted and grilled meats. This version is slightly less sweet than usual and will probably suit more tastes.

Serves 4

INGREDIENTS:

1 lb sweet potatoes
2 tbsp orange juice
1 tbsp maple syrup
Salt
3–4 tbsp vegetable or sunflower oil
1 tsp sesame seeds
Flat-leaf parsley to garnish

PREPARATION:

1. Preheat the oven to 400F.

2. Peel and cut the potatoes into wedges or large cubes and place them in a large bowl. Mix together the orange juice, syrup and a large pinch of salt and toss the potatoes in the mixture, coating them well.

3. Pour the oil into a medium roasting pan and place it in the oven until smoking hot. Add the potatoes to the oil and baste them well. Roast for 30–40 minutes, turning once or twice, until tender. If the potatoes seem to be browning too quickly, cover loosely with aluminum foil.

4. When ready to serve, transfer the potatoes to a warm serving dish, sprinkle with sesame seeds, and add a sprig or two of fresh parsley.

BAKED POTATOES WITH CORN AND CHICKEN

(above)

It is important to choose the right type of potato for baking. It should ideally be large and with a floury center, rather than a waxy type which is more suitable for salads. The Idaho would certainly fit the bill and can certainly be large enough (weighing 1lb or more), as can the Russet Burbank and Lemhi Russet, which are also good for mashing.

Serves 4

INGREDIENTS:

4 medium or 2 large baking potatoes in their skins

Vegetable oil
Salt and black pepper
$^1/_2$ cup cooked chicken, chopped
3 tbsp sweetcorn kernels
Parsley or chives to garnish

WHITE SAUCE:

2 tbsp butter
2 tbsp flour
$1^1/_4$ cups milk (warmed)

PREPARATION:

1. Preheat the oven to 400F. Scrub the potatoes, dry them, then prick them with a fork in a few places. Rub the skins well with oil and a little salt.

2. Place the potatoes on a rack in the oven and bake for about 1 hour or more, according to the size of the potatoes. Test by gently squeezing them with your fingers or piercing with a fork.

3. When the potatoes are tender, cut a cross in their tops and gently squeeze them from underneath to open them up.

4. Make the white sauce: melt the butter in a medium pan, beat in the flour to form a paste, then cook for 1 minute. Gradually blend in the warm milk and whisk as it comes to a boil to prevent lumps from forming. Beat well while cooking for 1–2 minutes. Season with salt and pepper. Stir the chicken and sweetcorn into the sauce and spoon this mixture back into the potatoes. Return the potatoes to the oven for about 20 minutes until thoroughly warmed through.

Tip: There are endless ways to vary this recipe. The white sauce could become a cheese sauce simply by adding a cup of grated cheese at the last minute and letting it melt into the sauce. Ham could be substituted for chicken. This could also be turned into a vegetarian dish by using any number of cooked vegetables, for example, broccoli or cauliflower, mixed with cheese sauce, stuffed into a baked potato and briefly placed under a hot broiler to brown.

WALDORF SALAD (below left)
This was created by Chef Oscar Tschirky at New York's Waldorf Astoria hotel in the 1890s, when it was considered the height of sophistication. The original version contained only apples, celery and mayonnaise, but walnuts and halved seeded grapes were added later.

Serves 4

INGREDIENTS:
1 red- and 1 green-skinned apple
1 tbsp lemon juice
3 sticks of celery, thinly sliced
1/2 cup walnuts, broken up
1/2 cup seedless red grapes, halved (optional)
1/4 cup good mayonnaise
1/4 cup sour cream
Salt and black pepper
Radicchio and endive leaves

PREPARATION:
1. Core and thinly slice the apples into a bowl and immediately toss in the lemon juice. Add the celery, the walnuts and the grapes if using them.

2. Blend the mayonnaise and sour cream together, then stir into the salad and mix well. Add seasoning to taste.

3. Serve on a bed of salad leaves.

POTATO SALAD (overleaf)
The best kind of potato for this popular dish is the waxy type, which does not crumble and can be sliced without falling to pieces. It is best to dress the salad when the potatoes are still warm, allowing the flavors to be immediately absorbed.

Serves 6

INGREDIENTS:
2 lb potatoes, scrubbed

1 small red onion, very finely chopped
1 stick of celery, chopped
¼ cup fresh chopped parsley
1 cup good mayonnaise
2 tbsp red wine vinegar
Salt and freshly ground black pepper
4 chopped scallions
Chopped chives

PREPARATION:
1. Boil the potatoes whole and when cool enough to handle remove their skins. If small, leave them whole, or cut them into smaller pieces. (If using new potatoes the skins can be left on.)

2. In a large bowl, mix together the onion, celery, parsley, scallions, mayonnaise and vinegar, then add the potatoes. Add salt and pepper and combine everything together thoroughly.

3. Garnish with a scattering of chopped chives.

MACARONI SALAD
Various pastas have interesting shapes and textures and because they have virtually no flavor of their own, like rice, couscous, bulgar and various grains, make the perfect base for sauces and whatever combination of ingredients you may choose.

Serves 4

INGREDIENTS:
2 red peppers
8 oz macaroni or spirals, cooked *al dente* in salted
  water
Basil

DRESSING:
3 tbsp olive oil
1 tbsp wine vinegar
1 clove of garlic, crushed
1 tsp dry mustard
Salt and black pepper
Pinch of sugar

PREPARATION:
1. Preheat the oven to 400F. Place the peppers on a sheet and bake until the skins begin to char and blister and the peppers become soft. Place the peppers in a plastic bag, tie it up, then let the steam do its work. When cool enough to handle, remove the skins and seeds from the peppers and cut them into thin strips. (Note that all this can be done ahead of time.)

2. Using a screw-top jar, shake together all the ingredients for the dressing to the consistency of light cream.

3. Place the pasta and peppers in a large bowl, pour on the dressing, and mix well. Garnish with torn basil.

CAESAR SALAD (right)
This American classic is thought to have been the creation of Chef Caesar Cardini at his restaurant in Tijuana, New Mexico in 1924, where it was made with whole leaves of romaine lettuce and eaten with the fingers. There are, of course, many variations and possible additions. Nowadays, there is some doubt concerning the safety of using raw eggs to thicken a salad dressing. If in doubt, use eggs which have first been coddled or lightly cooked.

Serves 4

INGREDIENTS:
1 head cos or romaine lettuce
2 eggs
1/2 cup olive oil
2 cloves of garlic, crushed
2–3 tbsp fresh lemon juice
Salt and black pepper
4–6 anchovy fillets, mashed to a paste
1/2 cup freshly grated Parmesan cheese
12–16 bread croutons

PREPARATION:
1. Wash and thoroughly dry the lettuce leaves, then tear them into strips or leave whole. Wrap them in paper towels and chill for as long as possible.

2. Break the eggs into a salad bowl and whisk well, then add the oil gradually in a thin stream, continuing to whisk until slightly thickened. Whisk in the garlic, lemon juice, seasoning and anchovies.

3. Add the lettuce and toss. Then add the Parmesan cheese and toss again. Add the croutons just before serving. As a variation, slices of hard-boiled eggs and bacon pieces can also be added .

Alternative Version: Place the eggs into a pan of boiling water, bring back to a boil and boil for 10 seconds. Remove and leave to stand for 1 minute. Toss the lettuce with the garlic, oil, seasoning and a little lemon juice. Carefully remove the shells from the eggs and break them directly into the salad. Add the anchovies and remaining lemon juice and mix well until the lettuce is well coated with the dressing. Finally, stir in the cheese and sprinkle in the croutons.

COLESLAW (below)
This raw cabbage salad, first brought to America by the Dutch, is a familiar and popular standby. Don't hesitate to add ingredients of your own, for example, shredded peppers, sliced apples or celery.

Serves 4

INGREDIENTS:
1/2 white cabbage, shredded
2 medium carrots, peeled and grated
1 small onion, thinly sliced
6 tbsp good mayonnaise
2 tbsp cider vinegar
1 tsp Dijon mustard
1/2 tsp caraway seeds (optional)
Salt and pepper

PREPARATION:
1. In a large bowl, mix together the cabbage, carrot and onion.

2. Blend together the mayonnaise, vinegar and mustard and stir into the salad. Add the caraway seeds, if using, and seasoning to taste.

3. Cover well and refrigerate for 1–2 hours before serving.

WARM CHICKEN SALAD WITH CREAMY DRESSING (page 45)
Warm salads are a West Coast favorite and variations on the theme are endless. In fact, warm scallops, grilled fresh tuna or swordfish, grilled bacon and sautéed kidneys or scallops are all delicious combined with raw salad vegetables and a flavorful dressing.

Serves 4

INGREDIENTS:
6 tbsp olive oil
2 boneless chicken fillets, cut through horizontally to give 4 thinner slices
1 carrot, cut into matchsticks
2 oz green cabbage or spinach, shredded
2 tbsp freshly cooked garden peas
1 large clove of garlic, thinly sliced
1 avocado, thinly sliced
1 tsp Dijon mustard
1 tsp lemon juice
1 tsp fresh chopped parsley
Salt and black pepper
2 tbsp heavy cream or crème fraîche
Cooked rice

PREPARATION:
1. Heat 3 tbsp oil in a small skillet and brown the chicken on all sides. Reduce the heat and continue until the chicken is cooked through. Transfer to a large bowl.

2. Add the rest of the oil to the pan with the carrot, cabbage, peas and garlic and cook over a fairly high heat until the cabbage wilts. Add the avocado, then transfer everything to the bowl with the chicken.

3. Stir the mustard, lemon juice, parsley and seasoning into the pan, then whisk in the cream.

4. Serve the chicken salad on a bed of warm cooked rice, spooning the dressing over it at the last minute.

CALIFORNIA SHRIMP SALAD (opposite)
Frozen shrimp is very good, but if you live near the coast fresh shrimp is sometimes available and you should not hesitate to buy it. You will certainly notice the difference in flavor.

Serves 1

INGREDIENTS:
3 oz raw shrimp
1 tbsp sunflower oil
1 tsp chili sauce
1 tbsp mayonnaise
1 tsp mild mustard
3 slices bacon, crisply cooked and chopped
3 tbsp sweetcorn kernels
1/4 green pepper, chopped
1/4 red pepper, chopped
1 tomato, seeded and chopped
2 tbsp canned black or cannellini beans, drained
1 tbsp chopped red onion
1/4 avocado, chopped and tossed in lemon juice

PREPARATION:
1. Heat the oil in a small pan and stir-fry the shrimp until it turns pink. Leave to cool, then shell and cut the shrimp in half.

2. Mix the chili sauce, mayonnaise and mustard together, then stir in the bacon.

3. Arrange all the ingredients in blocks on a large plate with the bacon-mayonnaise mixture in the center.

ADDITIONS AND FLAVORINGS:
Butter
Salt
Sugar
Finely grated cheese
Maple or corn syrup
Chili powder

PREPARATION:

1. Heat the oil in a large pan with a close-fitting lid, preferably with a steam vent. When the oil is hot, add one or two corn kernels and once they pop you can add the rest, but don't place more than a thin layer over the base of the pan at any one time.

2. Cover with the lid and return to the heat. Keep shaking the pan so that the corn does not burn. Once popping begins you will need to shake quite vigorously and frequently so that the corn is evenly cooked.

3. When the popping noise subsides you can then remove the lid, but not before, or you are likely to lose some on the floor. Add any flavorings, either savory or sweet, at the very last minute, then replace the lid and shake briefly to coat the popcorn.

4. Carefully transfer to a dish, discarding any unpopped or burnt kernels.

Tip: If you wish, you can make a caramel syrup in advance so that it is ready to add to the pan of popped corn. Dissolve 2 level tablespoons of light brown sugar with 2 tablespoons of unsalted butter and 1 tablespoon of milk or water.

HOLIDAY QUICHE (right)

Any favorite vegetable can be used in a quiche, or choose smoked salmon or shrimp as a special treat.
Serves 6

INGREDIENTS:
PASTRY:
6 oz all-purpose flour
Pinch of salt
3 oz butter
About 2 tbsp cold water

FILLING:
4 oz asparagus, trimmed

POPCORN (above)

Although you can buy popping corn ready to go into the microwave, making it from scratch at home is much more fun and often produces a better result. Allow 1–2 oz popping corn per person as you will find that it increases almost eightfold.

Serves 4
INGREDIENTS:
8 oz popping corn
1 tbsp vegetable oil

4 oz broccoli, broken into florets
2 scallions, chopped
3 eggs, beaten
1 cup light cream
2 cups Gruyère cheese, grated
1½ tsp salt
¼ tsp dried basil
Pepper

PREPARATION:

1. Sieve the flour and salt into a bowl, then rub the butter into the flour until the mixture resembles fine breadcrumbs.

2. Add just enough water to bring the mixture together into a ball. Cover with plastic wrap and refrigerate for 1 hour.

3. Cook the asparagus and broccoli in boiling salted water for 3 minutes, drain, then cut into small pieces. Set aside.

4. Preheat the oven to 350F.

5. Roll out the pastry and use it to line a 9-inch pie pan. Lightly prick the surface of the pastry, cover it with parchment and baking beans, and bake for 10 minutes. Remove the parchment and beans.

6. Place the asparagus and broccoli into the base of the pastry shell and sprinkle the scallions over. Beat the eggs and cream together, stir in the cheese, salt, basil and pepper and pour into the pastry shell.

7. Return to the oven for 25–30 minutes until the quiche is set and golden brown. Leave to stand for 10 minutes, then carefully remove from the pan. Serve warm or cold.

SHRIMP AND AVOCADO TORTILLAS (opposite)

This tasty combination, spiked with a touch of chili and lime, is served on a crisp tortilla base. It makes a delicious light meal or snack to eat at any time.
Serves: 4

INGREDIENTS:

½ each red and yellow peppers, thinly sliced
1 zucchini, washed and cut into matchsticks
1 small onion, sliced
20 large cooked shrimp
1 tbsp tomato or sundried tomato dressing
2 tbsp olive oil
Salt and black pepper
1 small ripe avocado
1 tbsp lemon juice
4 thin, crisp tortillas
½ iceberg lettuce, shredded
1–2 tbsp sour cream
1–2 tsp finely chopped red chilli
Cilantro leaves
1 lime, cut in thin wedges

PREPARATION:

1. In a bowl, mix together the peppers, zucchini, onion and shrimp.

2. Blend together the dressing, oil and seasoning with 1 tbsp iced water.

3. Thinly slice the avocado and toss it immediately in lemon juice.

4. To serve, place a tortilla on each plate. Add a few avocado slices, some shredded lettuce and the shrimp mixture. Then add a little dressing, a spoonful of sour cream, a sprinkling of chili, a few cilantro leaves and a wedge or two of lime.

BREADS & SANDWICHES

CORNBREAD

This important staple is served with many a simple dish. It can be made tastier by throwing in a handful of grated Parmesan cheese and extra seasoning or sweet by adding sugar. Serve warm with melted butter for breakfast or with soups or, as the Italians do polenta, with a casserole of game or wild mushrooms.

Serves 6–8

INGREDIENTS:
2 cups white or yellow cornmeal or polenta
1 cup all-purpose flour
1 tsp salt
2 tsp baking powder
2 large or 3 medium eggs, beaten together
6 tbsp butter, melted
1 cup milk

PREPARATION:
1. Lightly grease and line a shallow baking pan measuring approximately 9 x 11 inches. Preheat the oven to 375F.

2. In a large mixing bowl, combine all the dry ingredients. Make a hollow in the center, then gradually work in the eggs, melted butter and milk, beating well to produce a smooth batter.

3. Pour into the prepared pan and bake for about 20 minutes or until just firm. Remove from the oven and cool slightly before serving with butter or as you prefer.

Tip: To serve as a dessert, add 6 tablespoons of sugar to the other dry ingredients and serve warm, topped with maple syrup or cooked berries and heavy cream or ice cream.

HUSH PUPPIES

These are battered corn fritters that are traditionally served with fried fish. They can be flavored with cheese, onions, spices or even pecans.

Makes about 20

INGREDIENTS:
3 oz corn kernels, canned or frozen
$2/3$ cup all-purpose flour
$1^1/3$ cup cornmeal
2 tsp baking powder
$1/2$ tsp each red and black pepper
$1/2$–1 tsp salt
$1/2$ tsp each dried thyme and oregano
2 cloves of garlic, crushed
1 egg, beaten
1 cup milk, buttermilk or thin yogurt
Oil for frying

PREPARATION:
1. In a large bowl, mix together the corn and all the dry ingredients.

2. In a separate bowl, mix together the garlic, egg and milk. Stir this gently into the dry ingredients until lightly blended.

3. Heat 2 inches of oil in a deep frying pan, or use a deep-fryer with the correct amount of oil heated to 350F. Carefully drop small spoonfuls of the mixture into the pan and cook a few at a time so that there is plenty of space for them to move around.

4. When golden brown, remove with a slotted spoon and drain on paper towels. Serve sprinkled with a little salt.

CORN PONES

Also known as johnnycakes, these little corn biscuits are America's original cornbread, once made with only cornmeal, water and salt. They used to be cooked over an open fire until they were very crisp on the outside and still soft in the middle. They still make a popular snack, eaten broken open and spread with butter.

Makes 4

INGREDIENTS:
2 cups stone-ground cornmeal
1 tsp baking powder
$1/2$ tsp salt
$2/3$ cup water
$1/2$ cup milk
1 tbsp melted butter

PREPARATION:
1. Sift the cornmeal into a mixing bowl and stir in the

baking powder, salt, water and milk. Mix in the butter and leave for 10 minutes.

2. Preheat the oven to 375F and place a baking sheet inside. Take spoonfuls and, using your hands, shape the mixture into four or more pones or cup shapes.

3. Place the pones on the preheated tray and bake for 15–20 minutes until golden but not dried out. Serve immediately with butter.

CLASSIC BLUEBERRY AND BUTTERMILK MUFFINS

(pictured above, with chocolate muffin behind)
This is probably America's most famous muffin and the one most imitated abroad. Remember that the richer and sweeter the muffin the longer it stays moist, so this one certainly fits the bill!

Makes 6–8 large muffins

INGREDIENTS:
2 cups all-purpose flour
Pinch of salt
$1/2$ tsp baking soda
2 tsp baking powder
8 tbsp light brown sugar
2 eggs, beaten
$1/2$ tsp vanilla extract
$2/3$ cup buttermilk or natural yogurt
4 tbsp butter, melted
6 oz fresh blueberries

PREPARATION:
1. Sift the flour into a bowl with the other dry ingredients. Preheat the oven to 375F. Lightly grease a muffin pan or cups.

53

2. Beat the eggs with the vanilla, buttermilk and butter and stir these into the dry ingredients. Then stir in the blueberries, being careful not to break them up. Spoon the mixture into the muffin pan or cups.

3. Bake for 30 minutes or until risen and just firm. Allow to cool slightly before serving with thick crème fraîche, cream or simply on their own.

CRANBERRY AND ORANGE MUFFINS (left)

This is a wonderfully tangy variation on the muffin theme.

Makes 6–8

INGREDIENTS:
3 cups all-purpose flour
Generous 1/2 cup sugar
1 1/2 tsp baking powder
Pinch of salt
Few drops vanilla extract
1 egg, beaten
1/2 cup butter or margarine, melted
1/2 cup milk
2 tsp grated orange rind
8 oz dried cranberries
1 tbsp currants

PREPARATION:
1. Preheat the oven to 350F.

2. Sieve the flour into a large bowl with the sugar, baking powder and salt. Stir in the vanilla, egg, butter, milk and rind. Mix together lightly so that the mixture is just blended.

3. Fold in the cranberries and currants and spoon the mixture into muffin pans or cups. Bake for 20–25 minutes until well risen and just firm to the touch.

CALIFORNIA TEA LOAF

A vast quantity of top-quality dried fruit, famous the world over, is produced in the San Joaquin valley of California. Make this fruity tea bread for a quick and nutritious sunshine breakfast.

Serves 10

INGREDIENTS:
8 oz raisins
7–8 tbsp warm weak tea
1 1/2 cups all-purpose flour
1 tsp baking powder
Pinch of salt
2 tbsp butter or margarine
1/4 cup light brown sugar
1 large egg, beaten
Grated rind and juice of 1 large lemon
2 tbsp chopped walnuts or pecan nuts
Runny honey or brown sugar to finish

PREPARATION:
1. Preheat the oven to 350F. Line and lightly grease a 1-lb loaf pan.

2. Soak the raisins in the tea for 10–15 minutes. Sieve the flour, baking powder and salt together.

3. Cream the butter and sugar together, then gradually add the beaten egg. Stir in the flour mixture, raisins, lemon rind and juice and nuts and mix to a soft dropping consistency. Spoon into the pan and flatten the top.

4. Bake on the center rack of the oven for 45–50 minutes, brushing the top with honey or sprinkling it with sugar near the end of the cooking time.

5. When firm to the touch and golden, remove from the oven and leave to cool in the pan for 15 minutes. Remove and wrap in wax paper. Leave for a day or so to mature.

APPLE BUTTER (overleaf)

This is a thick, old-fashioned spread inspired by a well-known Shaker recipe. It is particularly delicious on warm scones, muffins or pancakes or spread on tea loaf.

Makes about 4 cups

INGREDIENTS:
5 lb tart apples (Bramleys or Baldwins, for example)
7 cups apple juice or sweet cider
1 1/2 cups light brown sugar
1 tbsp allspice
1/2 tsp salt

PREPARATION:
1. Wash the apples and cut them up fairly small without peeling or coring them. Put them into a preserving pan and cover with the liquid. (The original

recipe starts with four times the amount of apple juice or cider, which is then boiled down to the required quantity.)

2. Once the apples and liquid have come to a boil, reduce the heat and simmer gently, stirring from time to time until the apples reduce to a pulp. Strain the pulp through a sieve, then continue to cook until a spoon drawn through the mixture allows you to see the bottom of the pan. Stir constantly to avoid burning.

3. When the apple mixture is thick and darkly-colored, stir in the sugar, spice and salt, then pour into clean, warm jars. Cover, cool and refrigerate. Leave the apple butter for a week or so before using it, but don't keep it much longer than a couple of weeks.

AVOCADO AND CHICKEN DOUBLE-DECKER (right)

The club sandwich, or double-decker, is an all-American invention, found almost everywhere, from smart restaurants to diners, and dates from the late-nineteenth century. The bread is best toasted and allowed to dry out slightly before using. Foreign specialty breads, such as focaccia and ciabatta, can also be used.

Serves 4

INGREDIENTS:
12 slices white bread
Butter (optional)
2 hard-boiled eggs, shelled
4–5 tbsp mayonnaise
Salt and pepper
2 avocados
1 tbsp lemon juice
5–6 slices ham or smoked pork
Iceberg or bibb lettuce
10–12 pitted black olives, sliced
4 oz cooked chicken
Mustard cress

PREPARATION:
1. If you wish, butter the bread on one side only. Mash the eggs with the mayonnaise and seasoning. Slice one avocado and toss it in lemon juice. Mash the other avocado with salt and pepper.

2. Using three slices of bread for each sandwich, layer the fillings as follows: bread, mashed avocado, ham, avocado slices, bread, egg mayonnaise, lettuce, olive slices, chicken, cress and finally mashed avocado and the top layer of bread.

3. The sandwiches can be cut into triangles, wrapped in foil or plastic wrap and chilled before serving.

SAN FRANCISCO SOURDOUGH BREAD

Sourdough is one of the oldest and most natural forms of bread leavening. The San Francisco area was found to have a particular microclimate which encouraged certain wild yeasts crucial to the process. Its reputation grew during the Gold Rush era when prospectors took pieces of starter with them into the hills. Nowadays it is possible to buy sourdough starter kits or make your own using commercial yeast.

Makes 2 large loaves

INGREDIENTS:
SOURDOUGH STARTER:
$1/2$ oz fresh yeast or 1 tbsp dry yeast
2 cups warm water (or a mixture of water and natural
  low-fat yogurt)
1 tsp sugar
$2^1/2$ cups white bread flour

BREAD:
$3^1/3$ cups white bread flour
2 cups + 2 tbsp bottled water, slightly warmed
10 oz sourdough starter (at room temperature)
1 tbsp salt

PREPARATION:
1. To make the starter, dissolve the yeast in $1/4$ cup of
the warm water mixed with the sugar. Stir this into the
flour with more of the warm water to produce a
pourable batter. Cover with a damp cloth and leave in
a warm, draft-free place for 3–5 days to allow it to
ferment. (Whenever you use some of the starter you
must keep at least 1 cup back and replace this with as
much flour and water (equal quantities) as you have
used. The starter will also need "feeding" every 3–4
days by adding $1/4$ cup of flour and the same amount of
water.)

2. To make the bread, place the flour, water and
sourdough starter in a bowl and mix with a hand
whisk. Then cover with a damp cloth and leave in a
warm place for 4–5 hours until the dough begins to
bubble, indicating that the starter is doing its work.

3. Put this dough into a mixer with a dough hook and
add a further $1^2/3$ cups of flour. Beat gently until it
begins to come together, then beat for a further 5
minutes before adding the rest of the flour and the salt.
Now beat very slowly for a further 8 minutes.

4. Transfer the dough to a flat tray or large container,
sprinkle with flour, cover with a cloth, then leave in a
warm place for 1 hour. Then, with floured hands and
working on a floured surface, fold and knead the
dough briefly (three times or so). Cover with a clean
cloth and leave for a further 1 hour in a warm place.
Repeat this process twice more.

5. Finally, divide the dough into two, shape into long
loaves, dust with flour and leave on trays or in floured
loaf pans to prove for another 3–4 hours.

6. Preheat the oven to maximum and bake the loaves,
preferably side-by-side, in the center of the oven for 10
minutes.

7. Reduce the heat to 350F and bake for a further 40
minutes until a rich crust has formed and the loaves
sound hollow when tapped on their undersides.

NEW YORK BLT
*This must be the best-known of all sandwiches and of
course dozens of variations have evolved. Here are just
a few.*

Serves 1

INGREDIENTS:
2 slices fresh white bread, toasted and buttered
3–4 slices crisply-cooked smoked bacon
Iceberg lettuce
3–4 slices firm, ripe tomato

PREPARATION:
The original version consists simply of the above
ingredients layered and served between slices of
slightly warm bread. The Hard Rock Café version, also
thought to be the original, uses mayonnaise and
romaine lettuce, while some New York delis make it
with toasted sourdough bread and aïoli (garlic
mayonnaise). It has also been known for peanut butter,
grilled chicken or turkey, avocado or guacamole to be
added. Take your pick!

NEW YORK BAGELS (right)
*The bagel is synonymous with the New York deli,
where Hungarian, Italian, German, Jewish, Chinese,
and many more influences are in evidence. Fill your
bagel with whatever you fancy that day. Here are just a
few ideas.*

Fillings for 1 bagel

INGREDIENTS:
a) 1 tbsp cream cheese
   1 good slice smoked salmon (lox)
   Black pepper and a squeeze of lemon
b) 2 thin slices salami, pastrami or hot salt beef
   1–2 tbsp coleslaw

c) 1 large egg
    Salt and black pepper
    Knob of butter
    2 oz wild mushrooms
d) Thin slice of roasted or grilled eggplant
    1 tbsp guacamole, well spiked with chili
    Salad of arugula, spinach and red onion

PREPARATION:

a) Split the bagel and spread both halves with the
    cream cheese. Place the smoked salmon on one
    half, season with black pepper and lemon juice,

and top with the other half.

b) Split and spread the bagel with butter, then fill with
    slices of pastrami and the coleslaw.

c) Beat the egg with the seasoning. Heat the butter in
    a small omelet pan, then sauté the mushrooms until
    soft. Pour in the egg mixture. Cook gently until the
    egg is set, fold over into four, then place
    immediately between two halves of a buttered
    bagel.

d) Place a warm slice of eggplant on one half of a
    buttered bagel, spread with guacamole, top with
    salad and add the bagel top.

DESSERTS

APPLE PIE (opposite)
The all-American apple pie, with a crisp crust and a mound of spicy apple inside.

Serves 6–8

INGREDIENTS:
1 lb bought pastry
1/2 cup superfine sugar
1 tsp cinnamon
1/4 tsp each nutmeg and allspice
1 tbsp cornstarch
1 tsp lemon rind, cut into thin slivers
2 lb apples, peeled, quartered and the cores removed
1 tbsp egg white
1 tbsp superfine sugar

PREPARATION:
1. Preheat the oven to 400F. Line a deep 9-inch pie pan with about two-thirds of the pastry. Cover the remainder and set it aside for the lid.

2. Combine the sugar, cinnamon, nutmeg, allspice, cornstarch and lemon rind in a mixing bowl. Add the apples and mix well, then transfer the apples to the pie shell. Cover with the remaining pastry, sealing the edges with a little water.

3. Press the pastry edges neatly together and make a hole in the center. Beat the egg white with 1 tablespoon of water and brush it over the pastry, then sprinkle with a tablespoon of sugar.

4. Bake for 30 minutes, then reduce the heat to 350F and continue to bake for a further 20 minutes or until the fruit seems tender when a skewer is inserted. Remove from the oven and allow to cool slightly before serving with vanilla ice cream.

SHOOFLY PIE
This is a famous Pennsylvania Dutch specialty and so sweet, rich and delicious that you may well find yourself shooing everyone away from it!

Serves 6–8

INGREDIENTS:
1 7-inch pastry shell (can be bought)
1 cup molasses blended with 5–6 tbsp hot water

1 egg, beaten
1/2 tsp baking powder

TOPPING:
2 cups all-purpose flour
1/2 cup dark brown sugar
1/4 tsp each cinnamon and ginger
1/2 cup butter

PREPARATION:
1. Preheat the oven to 375F. Place the pastry shell on a baking sheet.

2. In a large mixing bowl combine together the dry ingredients for the topping and rub in the butter to form a crumbly texture.

3. Place the molasses and water, the egg and the baking powder in another bowl and beat together until blended. Pour the molasses mixture into the pastry shell, sprinkle on the topping, then bake for about 45 minutes until the topping is quite firm but the base, when you cut into the pie, is still moist. Serve warm with vanilla ice cream.

BERRY GRUNT
Old-fashioned early-American puddings and pies were often given names like grunt, buckle, slump – highly descriptive of the way they would sometimes collapse under the heat of an open fire. In other words, it didn't matter what the dish looked like as long as it tasted delicious – and it did!

Serves 4–5

INGREDIENTS:
2 cups blueberries
2 cups raspberries or blackberries
4 tbsp superfine sugar
1/2 cup light brown sugar
1 cup all-purpose flour
1/4 cup oats
1/2 cup unsalted butter
1/2 cup chopped pecans or walnuts
Confectioners' sugar

PREPARATION:
1. Wash and hull the fruit, drain, then place it in a pan with the superfine sugar. Cook for a few minutes until

the sugar dissolves. Transfer to an ovenproof dish. Preheat the oven to 350F.

2. Mix together the brown sugar, flour and oats, then rub in the butter and stir in the nuts. Sprinkle this mixture over the fruit in a thick layer, then bake for about 40 minutes until the fruit is bubbling and the topping has turned golden brown.

3. Sprinkle with confectioners' sugar and serve with English custard or ice cream.

KEY LIME PIE (opposite)

If you decide to use actual Key limes you will find that, though flavorful, they are quite small and you will need three times as many to yield the amount of juice you require. This recipe uses regular limes.

Serves 8

INGREDIENTS:
CRUMB CRUST:
10 oz graham crackers, finely crushed
5 oz butter
1 tbsp corn syrup

FILLING:
Finely grated rind and juice of 4 limes
15-oz can sweetened condensed milk
1 envelope (2¼ tsp) powdered gelatin
1¼ cups whipped cream

GARNISH:
Whipped cream
Lime slices

PREPARATION:
1. Place the crushed crackers in a bowl. Melt together the butter and syrup and pour it into the crackers. Mix well, then press the mixture into the base and up the sides of a 9-inch fluted pie pan. Chill until firm.

2. Mix together the grated rind and juice and the condensed milk, then chill.

3. Place the gelatin in a small bowl and pour on 2–3 tablespoons of very hot (not boiling) water. Stir until blended then microwave on full power in 15–20-second bursts, or place the bowl over a small pan of boiling water until the gelatin becomes quite clear. Stir into the milk mixture and mix thoroughly.

4. Fold the whipped cream into the lime filling. When lightly blended, spoon into the crumb crust and level the top. Chill for 3 hours until firm.

5. To serve, carefully transfer the pie from the pan to a serving dish. Pipe swirls of whipped cream around the edge and decorate with lime slices.

BAKED ALASKA

This stunning pudding was popularized at Delmonico's in New York in 1867, around about the time that William H. Seward bought Alaska from the Russians for about 2 cents an acre.

Serves 6

INGREDIENTS:
1 ready-made round or rectangular sponge cake (about 1 lb)
2¼ cups ice cream (whatever flavor you like)
3 large egg whites
6 oz superfine sugar
Fruit or mint to decorate

PREPARATION:
1. Cut the cake into 6 thick slices and arrange them back in the original shape of the cake on a heat- and freezer-proof plate. Spread the ice cream on top, following the shape of the cake and keeping the ice cream to within an inch of the cake edge all round. Freeze.

2. Whisk the egg whites until stiff, then gradually whisk in the sugar until the mixture is thick and glossy. Swirl the meringue mix over the ice cream and return the cake to the freezer until ready to cook.

3. When the dessert is required, preheat the oven to 220F. Allow the cake 5–10 minutes to defrost, then bake for only about 5 minutes or until the meringue just begins to turn golden. Decorate if you wish and serve immediately.

Tip: To flambé, warm 3–4 tablespoons of brandy or other liqueur in a small pan or ladle. Pour the brandy around the base of the Baked Alaska and ignite it immediately before serving.

SPELLBINDING PUMPKIN PIE (left)

It should be remembered that although this contains a vegetable purée it is really a custard pie. Be careful not to overcook it; remove it from the oven when it is still wobbly. The pie will continue to firm up as it cools.

Serves 10

INGREDIENTS:
PASTRY:
1¼ cups all-purpose flour
Pinch of salt
½ cup butter or margarine
About 2 tbsp cold water

FILLING:
3 eggs, separated
2 cups canned pumpkin purée
½ cup plus 2 tbsp sugar
1 cup sour cream
1 tsp cinnamon
¼ tsp ground ginger
¼ tsp ground nutmeg
¼ tsp ground cloves
¼ tsp salt

GARNISH:
⅔ cup whipped cream
½ cup pecans, roughly chopped

PREPARATION:
1. Place the flour and salt in a bowl, add the butter or margarine and rub it into the flour until it resembles fine breadcrumbs. Add the water and knead the mixture into a ball. Cover with plastic wrap and refrigerate for 1 hour.

2. Preheat the oven to 400F. Roll out the pastry and use it to line a 9-inch cake pan.

3. Whisk the egg whites until they form soft peaks. Beat together the egg yolks, pumpkin, sugar, sour cream, spices and salt until blended, then fold in the egg whites. Spoon the mixture into the pastry shell and bake for 10 minutes. Reduce the temperature to 350F and continue to bake for about 30 minutes or until the filling is just set and the crust golden brown.

4. Remove from the oven and leave to cool, then refrigerate until required. Remove the pie from the pan, place on a serving dish, then pipe the top with a circle of cream. Decorate with the pecans.

MISSISSIPPI MUD PIE (overleaf)

Sometimes called Chocolate Pie, this is also called Black Bottom Pie because of the rich, dark chocolate base and wickedly sticky filling.

Serves 8

INGREDIENTS:
PIE SHELL:
8 oz graham crackers or gingersnaps, crushed
1 oz cocoa powder
3 oz butter or margarine
3 tbsp maple syrup

FILLING:
¾ cup butter
1¼ cups dark brown sugar
4 large eggs
4 tbsp cocoa powder
5 oz plain chocolate, melted
1¼ cups light cream
1 tsp vanilla extract

MERINGUE:
2 large egg whites
1 cup confectioners' sugar
Sifted confectioners' sugar
Chocolate shavings

PREPARATION:
1. To make the pie shell, melt the cocoa, butter and syrup together and blend well, then add the crushed cookies. Press the mixture evenly into the base and up the sides of a 9-inch fluted cake pan. Preheat the oven to 375F.

2. For the filling, cream together the butter and sugar, gradually beat in the eggs with the cocoa powder, then stir in the melted chocolate followed by the cream and vanilla extract.

3. Spoon the filling into the pie shell and bake for about 35 minutes until almost set. Reduce the oven temperature to 325F.

Serves 6–8

INGREDIENTS:
PASTRY:
3 cups all-purpose flour
$1/2$ cup butter, cut into small pieces
2 oz ground almonds
2 tbsp superfine sugar

FILLING:
$1^1/2$ lb blueberries
$1/4$ tsp ground cinnamon
8 tbsp superfine sugar
2 tbsp arrowroot

PREPARATION:
1. Sift the flour into a mixing bowl and add the butter. Rub together gently with your fingertips until the mixture resembles fine breadcrumbs. Stir in the ground almonds and sugar and enough cold water to form a soft dough.

2. Preheat the oven to 400F. On a lightly floured surface, roll the pastry out and line a deep 8-inch flan or pie pan. Cover the pastry shell with a piece of baking parchment and heap baking beans on top.

3. Roll the pastry trimmings out thinly and use a cutter to make about 8 star shapes. Place them on a small cookie sheet to bake along with the pastry shell.

4. Cook the pastry shell and the stars for 10 minutes or until the pastry is golden and crisply cooked through. (Watch that the stars do not become too brown.)

5. Place the blueberries and cinnamon in a pan with the superfine sugar and simmer very gently until tender and the juice begins to flow.

6. Blend the arrowroot with a little water to form a smooth paste and mix it into the blueberries. Stir carefully over a gentle heat until the juice thickens to a syrupy consistency. Sprinkle with a little sugar to prevent a skin from forming and cool.

7. Spoon the fruit into the pastry shell, arrange the stars on top, then chill until quite set and very cold. Serve, cut into thick slices, with whipped cream or ice cream.

4. Whisk the egg whites until stiff, then gradually whisk in the sugar until the mixture is thick and glossy and holds in peaks. Place on top of the warm filling, using a spoon to make peaks on the surface, and return to the oven for 10–15 minutes, or until the meringue is cooked but not too brown.

5. Allow to cool and serve warm or cold with confectioners' sugar sifted over and chocolate shavings on top.

BLUEBERRY PIE (right)
Pies came to America with the Pilgrims and we have been having a love affair with them since. Ice cream goes particularly well with hot fruit pies, the contrast in temperature adding greatly to the enjoyment.

ICE CREAM SODA (below)

The traditional ice cream soda is still a beloved treat! The addition of chocolate is surprisingly delicious.

Serves 1

INGREDIENTS:
Chilled soda
1–2 scoops vanilla ice cream
Chocolate flakes

PREPARATION:
Fill a high-ball glass with ice and soda. Top with scoops of ice cream and chocolate flakes and drink through a straw. Alternatively, blend everything to a creamy froth in a food processor.

MARBLED STRAWBERRY CHEESECAKE (right)

Pretty as a picture and as delicious as it looks, this is an elegant dessert worthy of a special occasion.

Serves 8–10

INGREDIENTS:
CRUMB CRUST:
12 shortbread cookies
6 tbsp unsalted butter
3 oz dark chocolate

STRAWBERRY MARBLING:
1 envelope (2$\frac{1}{4}$ tsp) powdered gelatin
12 oz fresh strawberries, rinsed and hulled
2 tbsp superfine sugar
1 tbsp fraise or kirsch liqueur

FILLING:
1 envelope (2$\frac{1}{4}$ tsp) powdered gelatin
1$\frac{1}{4}$ lb cream cheese
3–4 drops vanilla extract
$\frac{1}{2}$ cup superfine sugar
3 cups softly whipped cream

PREPARATION:
1. Lightly butter a 9-inch springform cake pan and line it with oiled parchment.

2. Finely crush the cookies. Gently melt the butter and chocolate together and stir until smooth, then mix into the crumbs. Press the mixture evenly into the base of the pan and leave to thicken.

3. For the strawberry marbling, sprinkle the gelatin onto 4 tablespoons of hot water in a small bowl and dissolve in a microwave or over a small pan of hot water until clear.

4. Set aside one or two fine strawberries for decoration, then blend the rest with the sugar and liqueur and strain to remove the seeds. Whisk in the gelatin and place in the fridge until it begins to set.

5. For the cheesecake filling, sprinkle the gelatin onto 4 tablespoons of very hot water in a small bowl and dissolve it in a microwave or over a small pan of hot water. Blend the cream cheese, vanilla and sugar together, then whisk in the gelatin and fold in the cream.

FILLING:
Juice and grated rind of 1 large or 2 small lemons
1 envelope (2¹/₄ tsp) powdered gelatin
1 lb 2 oz cream cheese
¹/₂ cup superfine sugar
Scant cup heavy cream
9 oz fresh or defrosted raspberries

PREPARATION:
1. Mix the crushed crackers, sugar, ginger and melted butter together thoroughly and press the mixture evenly over the base and up the sides of a 9-inch springform cake pan. Leave to chill.

2. Place the lemon juice in a small bowl, sprinkle on the gelatin and heat until dissolved, either in a microwave or over a small pan of hot water. Stir until there are no lumps left and the mixture is completely clear.

3. Thoroughly blend the cream cheese, sugar and lemon rind together. Then gently stir in the gelatin mix.

6. When the strawberry mixture is thick enough, first spoon the cheesecake mixture over the crumb crust, then add spoonfuls of the strawberry mixture and gently swirl them together. Avoid stirring too much or you will lose the marbled effect. Chill for 1–2 hours before serving topped with a few sliced strawberries.

LEMON CHEESECAKE WITH RASPBERRIES (right)
New York is the home of the original American lemon cheesecake. Here it is with the added surprise of a layer of raspberries running through the middle.

Serves 8–10

INGREDIENTS:
CRUMB CRUST:
9 oz graham crackers, finely crushed
3 tbsp superfine sugar
¹/₂ tsp ground ginger
¹/₂ cup butter, melted

Whip the cream slightly and fold it in. Spoon half the mixture into the prepared crumb crust, sprinkle on the raspberries, keeping some back for decoration, then spoon in the rest of the filling mixture.

4. Chill for 1–2 hours. Decorate the top with the reserved raspberries.

AUTUMN FRUIT COBBLER (opposite)

Use whatever combination of orchard fruits, berries or currants you wish, but blackcurrants give a welcome tartness to what is quite a sweet dish.

Serves 4

INGREDIENTS:
12 oz firm apples or pears, peeled and sliced
12 oz hulled berries or currants, washed and dried
4–6 tbsp superfine sugar

COBBLER TOPPING:
2 cups flour, sieved
1 tsp baking powder
4 tbsp butter
4 tbsp superfine sugar
4–5 tbsp milk
2 tbsp yogurt

PREPARATION:
1. Mix the fruits with the sugar in a deep ovenproof dish. Place in the oven set at 375F while preparing the topping.

2. Sieve the flour and baking powder into a bowl, then rub in the butter. Add the sugar, then stir in 3–4 tablespoons of milk and the yogurt to give a soft dough. Roll out on a lightly floured surface to about 1/2-inch thick and cut into 8–10 small circles.

3. Turn the oven up to 425F. Arrange the circles of dough, slightly overlapping, over the top of the fruit and brush with a little milk. Bake for 20–25 minutes, turning down the heat if the cobbler topping seems to be getting too brown. When the topping is just firm, remove from the oven and serve, sprinkled with a little more superfine sugar.

CARROT CAKE

This is one cake you may be able to claim is good for you, while conveniently forgetting all the other

ingredients that are not so healthy. It is very moist and delicious and will keep well for several days – if you can resist it that long.

Serves 16

INGREDIENTS:
2/3 cup sunflower oil
Scant cup light brown sugar
3 large eggs, beaten
Finely grated rind and juice of one orange
1 1/2 cups wholegrain flour
1 tsp baking powder
6 oz raisins
6 oz carrots, peeled and finely grated

TOPPING:
4 oz low fat cream cheese
Superfine sugar to taste
Shredded orange rind

PREPARATION:
1. Preheat the oven to 350F.

2. Blend the cake ingredients together thoroughly but lightly, using only half the orange juice. Spoon the mixture into a lightly greased and lined 12 x 9-inch cake pan.

3. Bake for 40–50 minutes until the cake is risen and just firm to the touch. Leave to cool in the pan.

4. Blend the cream cheese with the remaining orange juice and sugar to taste to a piping or spreading consistency. Spread it evenly over the top of the cake and feather with a fork. Decorate with orange rind.

CHOCOLATE FUDGE BROWNIES (overleaf)

America invented brownies and now everyone loves them, which is not surprising once you've tasted them. Serve them warm.

Makes 16 squares

INGREDIENTS:
3/4 cup soft margarine
Scant cup dark brown sugar
2 eggs, beaten
1–2 tbsp corn or maple syrup

2 tbsp cocoa powder, sifted
Scant cup wholegrain flour
2 tsp ground ginger

TOPPING:
5 oz dark chocolate, broken into pieces
6 tbsp light brown sugar
4 tbsp margarine
$2/3$ cup heavy cream

PREPARATION:
1. Preheat the oven to 350F. Grease and line a deep 7-inch-square cake pan.

2. Cream together the margarine and sugar until fluffy. Add the eggs, syrup and the dry ingredients, then blend together until smooth. Spoon the mixture into the pan and level the top. Bake for 35–40 minutes or until firm. Leave to cool in the pan.

3. Melt the chocolate, sugar and margarine for the topping together, stir in the cream, then cook gently for 1–2 minutes, stirring constantly.

4. Cut the warm brownies into squares and pour on the chocolate sauce.

5. To serve cold, leave the brownies in the pan and allow both brownies and sauce to cool, then spread or swirl the sauce over the top of the brownies. Cut into squares.

ANGEL FOOD CAKE

This American classic is a dieter's dream – no fat, no cholesterol, and not too many calories! And it is not difficult to make. Although little is known of its origins, the cake has been popular thoughout America since the late-nineteenth century. This light-as-a-feather confection deserves an elegant finish, so a choice of decorations is given.

Serves 18–20

INGREDIENTS:
5 tbsp flour, sifted
1 tbsp cornstarch
Generous cup superfine sugar
10 large egg whites
1 tsp cream of tartar

$1^1/2$ tsp vanilla extract
FROSTING:
$1/2$ cup superfine sugar
2 large egg whites
2 tsp corn syrup
$1/2$ tsp vanilla extract

DECORATION:
a) Shredded rind of 1 orange
b) 8 oz fresh raspberries and mint leaves
c) 2 oz dark chocolate curls

PREPARATION:
1. Preheat the oven to 350F. Sift the flour, cornstarch and $1/4$ cup of sugar into a large bowl. Do this three times to incorporate as much air as possible.

2. Using an electric whisk, beat the egg whites with the cream of tartar in a large, perfectly clean bowl until stiff. Gradually whisk in the rest of the sugar, a little at a time, until the mixture becomes thick and glossy.

3. Gently fold in the flour mixture and vanilla extract until evenly blended, then transfer to a 10-inch ring mold (do not grease). Bake for 35–40 minutes until well risen and golden on top. Turn the cake out onto a wire rack and leave to cool.

4. For the frosting, heat the sugar with 4 tablespoons of water in a small pan until the sugar dissolves. Boil the syrup until it reaches 240F on a sugar thermometer.

5. Whisk the egg whites until very stiff and dry, then slowly pour in the hot syrup, whisking all the time until the mixture becomes thick and glossy. Beat in the vanilla extract and continue beating for a further 5 minutes until the frosting has cooled down.

6. Transfer the cake to a serving dish and spread the frosting all over, making a swirly pattern with a knife. Decorate as you like and serve. The cake will store well in an airtight tin, but do not leave it in a damp place or the frosting will begin to sweat.

CHOCOLATE CHIP COOKIES (overleaf)
For the true chocoholic, these are a must!

Makes 20

INGREDIENTS:
$1/2$ cup unsalted butter, softened

4 tbsp sugar
Scant 1/2 cup light brown sugar
1 large egg, beaten
1/2 tsp vanilla extract
11/2 cups flour
l tsp baking powder
4 oz plain chocolate chips
4 oz white chocolate chips

PREPARATION:

1. Preheat the oven to 350F. Get two large cookie sheets ready.

2. In a large mixing bowl, cream together the butter and two sugars until light and fluffy. Gradually add the beaten egg, mixing after each addition, then beat in the vanilla extract.

3. Sift the flour and baking powder into the bowl and fold in thoroughly. Fold in the chocolate chips, then place heaped teaspoons of the mixture 2 inches apart onto the cookie sheets.

4. Bake for 10–12 minutes until golden. Allow to cool on the cookie sheets for 5 minutes, then transfer to a rack to cool completely.

Tip: If preferred, leave out half the chocolate and use chopped nuts to make up the weight.

S'MORES

These classic campfire treats will take you back to your younger days. You don't need a campfire to make them, though. You can roast the marshmallows on wooden sticks over any open flame: a fire in the fireplace or a barbecue grill.

Serves 4

INGREDIENTS:
4 large graham crackers
2 bars of chocolate
4–8 marshmallows

PREPARATION:

1. Break the graham crackers in half so that there is a top and bottom for each s'more. Break the bars of chocolate in half and lay each piece on a graham cracker half.

2. Put the marshmallows on the ends of wooden sticks, using 1–2 per person. (Don't use unbent coat hangers;

the metal gets hot.) Roast the marshmallows over an open flame until they are done to your liking. (Some like to roast them slowly. Some like to stick them directly in the flame so that the outside is burnt and the inside melted.)

3. Place the marshmallow on its stick between the top and bottom graham crackers and the chocolate. Hold onto the graham crackers and pull the stick out to avoid touching the hot marshmallows and burning your fingers.

STRAWBERRY SHORTCAKE (overleaf)

Strawberries are classic, but any soft fruits can be substituted as well as sweetened crème fraîche or a mixture of half sour cream, half regular cream.

Serves 8

INGREDIENTS:
11/2 cups butter, softened
1 scant cup superfine sugar
21/3 cups flour, sifted
1cup cornstarch, sifted
8 oz strawberries, hulled and wiped
11/4 cups whipped cream
1/2 cup flaked almonds, toasted
1 tsp confectioners' sugar, sifted

PREPARATION:

1. Work the butter, sugar, flour and cornstarch gently together using your fingertips, then turn onto a floured surface and knead the pastry briefly until smooth.

2. Cut the pastry in half and roll out each piece to make 8-inch circles, using a fluted cutter if possible. Lay on cookie sheets and chill for 10 minutes. Preheat the oven to 325F.

3. Bake the pastry circles for 55 minutes. When firm but not browned, remove from the oven. Cut the best-looking circle into eight triangles for the top and cool.

4. Halve the strawberries. Place the uncut shortcake on a serving dish and pipe on the cream. Place the strawberries on top, then fan out the triangles on top.

5. Scatter on the almonds and sprinkle with confectioners' sugar before serving.

MARBLE CAKE WITH DRIZZLE TOPPING (below)

A quick-and-easy family cake that will disappear almost as soon as you can cut it. Why not make two and keep one in the freezer?

INGREDIENTS:

3/4 cup soft margarine
Generous cup superfine sugar
3 large eggs
1 1/2 cups all-purpose flour
1 1/2 tsp baking powder
2 tbsp milk
2 drops vanilla extract
1 oz cocoa powder, sifted

TOPPING:

1 oz dark bitter chocolate
2 tbsp dark brown sugar
2 tbsp milk or cream

PREPARATION:

1. Preheat the oven to 350F. Line a 7–8-inch cake pan with non-stick baking parchment.

2. Cream together the margarine and sugar until light and fluffy, then gradually beat in the eggs, one at a time. Fold in the flour and baking powder and 1–2 tablespoons of milk.

3. Transfer half the mixture into another bowl. Add vanilla essence to one bowl and the cocoa plus a little more milk to the other bowl and mix both in gently.

4. Spoon the mixtures alternately into the pan until both mixtures are used up, then level the surface. Bake for 45–50 minutes, or until well-risen and a skewer inserted into the middle comes out clean. Turn out on to a wire rack and leave to cool.

5. Meanwhile, melt the chocolate, sugar and cream together and stir until blended. Allow to cool slightly then pour over the still-warm cake and leave until completely cold before cutting it.

CHOCOLATE ICE CREAM (opposite)

The ultimate chocolate ice cream – served with a rich chocolate syrup.

Serves 4

INGREDIENTS:
4 egg yolks
6 tbsp superfine sugar
1¼ cups milk
1 oz cocoa powder, sifted
4 oz dark chocolate
1¼ cups heavy cream, softly whipped

CHOCOLATE SYRUP:
4 tbsp maple syrup
1 tbsp rum or whisky
3 oz dark chocolate

PREPARATION:
1. Beat the egg yolks and sugar until pale, creamy and thick. Bring the milk just up to a boil, whisk in the cocoa powder, then add the chocolate. Stir until dissolved.

2. Pour the milk and chocolate into the egg mixture, whisking well. Sieve into a bowl over a pan of hot water and stir all the time as the custard begins to thicken. Remove from the heat and whisk occasionally as it cools.

3. When the chocolate custard is cool, fold in the softly whipped cream, pour into a freezer container, then cover with a lid or foil. Freeze, whisking every hour or so until too firm to continue, or mix in an ice cream machine for about 20 minutes before transferring it to a freezer container. Freeze for 3–4 hours. Allow 15 minutes for the ice cream to soften before serving.

4. Warm the syrup, rum and chocolate gently together until blended and serve warm with the ice cream.

FRUIT PANCAKES

Large or small fruit pancakes always make a popular dessert. They can be made in advance and frozen, individually wrapped, so that they are ready to defrost when needed.

Makes about 12

INGREDIENTS:
1½ cups all-purpose flour, sieved
Pinch of salt
1 tbsp sugar
2 eggs
1 cup milk
2 oz blueberries, blackberries or dried currants, cranberries or cherries
1 tsp baking soda
1 tsp baking powder
Few drops vanilla extract
Oil for frying

PREPARATION:
1. Mix together the flour, salt and sugar. Beat together the eggs and milk, stir them into the flour mixture and beat to a smooth, thickish batter.

2. Beat in the baking soda, baking powder and vanilla extract. Cover tightly and leave for at least ½ hour then, when ready to cook, stir in the fruit.

3. Heat a little oil in a non-stick heavy-based skillet, pancake pan or griddle. Drop 2 tablespoons of batter at a time onto the very hot surface and let it find its own level.

4. Leave the pancakes to cook over a high heat until bubbling on top and golden underneath, then carefully turn them over using a spatula. Cook for another 1–2 minutes on the other side, then transfer to a heated plate and keep warm while you cook the rest.

5. To serve, layer the pancakes with syrup or honey and serve hot with ice cream and more syrup.

INDEX